Edward Howard House

Japanese Episodes

Edward Howard House

Japanese Episodes

ISBN/EAN: 9783337171070

Printed in Europe, USA, Canada, Australia, Japan

Cover: Foto ©Andreas Hilbeck / pixelio.de

More available books at **www.hansebooks.com**

JAPANESE EPISODES

BY

EDWARD H. HOUSE

BOSTON
JAMES R. OSGOOD AND COMPANY
1881

STEREOTYPED AND PRINTED
BY RAND, AVERY, AND COMPANY,
BOSTON.

PREFATORY NOTE.

THE purpose of this little volume is to represent a few social and physical features of Japan which have seldom been minutely examined by visitors to that agreeable country. Its ingenious products are familiar to every connoisseur; its students have travelled and dwelt among us in sufficient numbers to give all who desire it the opportunity of making their acquaintance; and our libraries are well supplied with books descriptive of its history and politics. But of the inner life of the Japanese, of their domestic relations, their pleasures, or the gentler romance of their nature, I have found no accurate record. Nor has the singular loveliness of the scenery, the refining charm of which deeply influences the character of the people, been closely or sympathetically observed. Upon these points I have been so frequently questioned as to warrant the belief that the following recitals may take their modest place among the numerous memorials of Oriental experience, without peril of rejection as superfluous or intrusive. Necessarily, they touch but lightly on the themes indicated, and open a merely introductory view to the broad field they venture to approach; but, if they lead the way to more enterprising exploration hereafter, they will accomplish much of what their writer most earnestly desires. One of the sketches endeavors to portray the simple vicissitudes of rustic society, with the varying course of love in humble life; every detail of which is authentic, although fiction may have helped to weave together the several facts. Another deals solely with the scenic beauties of a region easily accessible by tourists. A third narrates the interchange of hospitalities between foreigners and natives in official "high life;" and the last sets forth a form of popular amusement in which all classes participate, and which exemplifies the genial, happy, and contented spirit of the community. To lead my own countrymen to a just appreciation of this pleasant land, and of those who inhabit it, has been my self-assigned task for many years; and I shall be gratified if the pictures here offered can contribute, in their unpretending way, to the realization of that end.

CONTENTS.

	PAGE
LITTLE FOUNTAIN OF SAKANOSHITA . . .	7
TO FUZIYAMA AND BACK	70
A JAPANESE STATESMAN AT HOME . . .	155
A DAY IN A JAPANESE THEATRE . . .	200

LITTLE FOUNTAIN OF SAKANO-SHITA.

I.

THE honorable gentleman is fond of beautiful scenery."

" Very fond of such scenery as this."

" Ah! He will find it much better as we go forward."

" Indeed!"

" Truly, among the mountains it is surprising. May I ask where the gentleman will stop tonight?"

" It does not matter; anywhere in this neighborhood."

" Has he (*danna san*) heard of Sakanoshita?"

" Never."

" Clearly not. Nobody — no foreigner — has ever visited it. At least, none has ever stopped there."

" Is it remarkable?"

" Noblest sir, it is wonderful. Not because I

live there; no, in truth. It is the universal report. Everybody will say the same of Sakanoshita."

"Then, how far are we now from it?"

"One *ri* and eighteen *cho.*"

"That is about an hour and a half in time. Very well: we will stay there, I suppose."

"Thanks! Really many thanks! It will not be possible to regret it. There is nothing like Sakanoshita."

This conversation took place at three o'clock in the afternoon, — a brilliant August afternoon, — in a pretty village on the road from Kuwana, the north-western port of the Bay of Ise, to Oötsu, at the south-western extremity of Lake Biwa; which ancient thoroughfare anybody may easily find upon a good-sized map of Japan. My informant and adviser was one of the lads who drew my *jin-riki-sha* (man-power-carriage), — a species of vehicle, which, first seen in Tokio in the fall of 1870, had in less than two years come into universal use in every part of the country where the roads were sufficiently level to render it practicable. It was little better than a cushioned chair upon a pair of wheels, but, compared with the old-fashioned *kago* which it displaced, was a triumph of luxury and convenience. By

Little Fountain of Sakanoshita. 9

its aid the discomforts of travelling in the interior, except among the mountainous regions, had been almost entirely banished.

My leading "power-man" had for some time been attracted by the attention I had given to the growing beauties of the landscape, and had from time to time offered such passing information as it was in his power to bestow, with the simple freedom, which, among the humbler Japanese, is never aggressive, and almost always welcome. On the other hand, his cheery humor, and the slight outward superiority to the average of his fellows which he exhibited, had recommended him to my notice at moments when I was not engaged in contemplating nature on a larger scale. He was an excellent specimen of his class, stalwart, alert, and full of a natural, easy grace. Many a Japanese workingman is a very fair Apollo between the ages of fifteen and twenty-five, and after that he becomes a respectable Hercules. If European and American painters and sculptors want masculine models which they will not need to idealize, they may import them in abundance from that distant land, and from nowhere else in these days, that I am aware of. This runner of mine was apparently a little over twenty; and besides possessing all the good points of an antique statue, with vitality thrown in, had certain distinguishing marks not likely to escape observation. His costume was primitive enough: but his waist-cloth, instead of being plain, as is generally the case, was of fanciful red-and-blue stuff; and, which was very unusual, he wore cloth *tabi* (half shoes, half socks), and not the customary rough straw sandals. From these trifling indications I gathered that he had a soul above the sordid considerations of his craft; and as I observed that he was occasionally addressed by his comrades, half satirically, yet not with evil humor, as *date-sha*, or dandy, it was clear, that, in spite of the limited capabilities of costume which he enjoyed, he had won a certain social fame in his humble sphere. And I afterward discovered, that, among the simple mountaineers of Ise, he was quite as clearly the glass of fashion as he was indisputably the mould of form.

Before we started forward from the wayside cottage I questioned him further: —

"Is there a good inn at Sakanoshita?"

"Many, sir, many. It was once a famous resting-place. In the old days it was almost always filled with noble lords. Yes, there are many inns; but there is one more excellent than all the others."

His listening fellows chuckled, upon which he

Little Fountain of Sakanoshita. 11

grew extremely red, but with confusion rather than with anger.

"And which is that?" I asked.

"The Fuku-ya," he answered, glowing from his waistband to the extremest point of his shaven crown, — the most comprehensive and unbroken blush that I ever had the opportunity of beholding.

The others laughed aloud, and he himself broke into a smile.

"Why do they laugh?"

As he gave no immediate answer, his partner for the day came forward, and explained: "*Danna San*, he speaks of 'the Fuku-ya,' because it is there that Koïzumi dwells."

"Indeed! Then, who is Koïzumi?"

"Koïzumi is the daughter of the house."

"She is a friend of mine," added my pleasant colloquist, who had recovered his equanimity with characteristic rapidity.

"A very pretty girl, no doubt."

"*Sayo de gozarimasu!*" assented the entire body of *jin-riki-sha* men in emphatic unison.

"Come, this is really interesting," said I. "We will certainly pass the night at Sakanoshita, and we will assuredly establish ourselves at the Fuku-ya; and, if we are fortunate, we will make the acquaintance of Koïzumi. That is settled. Forward — *Hayau!*"

We soon reached the edge of the mountains, and commenced an upward course which threatened to calm the impetuosity of some of our draft-men. But my young adviser seemed insensible to fatigue, and his spirits rose with the physical ascent. No amount of hard labor can ever conquer the good-humor of a Japanese workman; and as we drew near our destination the entire party burst out into loud cries, and increased their pace until they had whirled us almost headlong to the gates of a stately but somewhat timeworn *yado-ya*,[1] at the entrance of which, summoned doubtless by the approaching tumult, stood the landlady and her household, smiling and bowing as if our arrival had been the one ardently hoped-for event of their existence.

A few minutes later we were lying on the soft mats of the best apartment — the *daimio's* room, we were explicitly informed — that the inn afforded, and gazing with genuine delight upon one of the loveliest scenes that this land of beauty contains. But it was still early in the day; and, as the journey had been less exhausting than

[1] Inn: literally, shelter-enclosure.

Little Fountain of Sakanoshita. 13

usual, an exposition of activity fastened itself upon me. I announced a determination first to investigate the culinary resources of the establishment, and next to explore the village. I do not now pretend to deny, what I did not then affirm, that a willingness to get a glimpse of the vaunted daughter of the house had some share in urging me forth. As I passed slowly through the kitchen, scrutinizing its appointments with, I flatter myself, well-affected earnestness, I observed a rosy-cheeked young girl engaged in rapid discourse with my favorite runner. Well, she was certainly pretty enough : there was no danger of disappointment in that direction. My presence was at first unnoticed, and I was greatly entertained to hear the manner in which I was heralded by the enthusiastic and imaginative youth. "A very noble gentleman," he declared ; "a gentleman of the highest possible foreign rank ; a great lord ; a celebrated officer of the government ; a mountain of dignity and a river of affluence ; one thousand *riyos* a month, no less, I know it, and have seen it, — have seen it with these eyes ; " and an infinite deal more to the same fanciful effect. He was enjoying his brilliant fictions to such an extent, that I had not the heart to interrupt him, and passed out by a side passage, leaving him to the benefit of the impression he was endeavoring to produce by wildly exaggerating the importance of one of the guests he had introduced to the house.

A short ramble, a wholesome plunge into a mountain stream, and supper from imported tins, wound up the chapter of that day. Then early bed, and sound repose, in spite of casual and not wholly inanimate interruptions; dreams soothed to gentle images by the music of a hundred brooks and myriads of chirping *semi*, whose voices are heard only in the forests of Japan.

Such a breezy, hearty, radiant next morning! — a morning suited to the place; the very day, of all summer days, for a tramp over and about the valley. The young *jin-riki-sha* man should be our guide. Let him appear. What ho! — and so forth.

We had not risen; but thus early was the plan of the day determined upon. Again we shouted; but no familiar voice was heard in response. Presently, however, a sliding door was pushed aside; and a pair of bright eyes — the eyes of Koïzumi — looked in upon us.

"By Jove!" exclaimed my travelling companion, whom I have discourteously omitted to mention until this moment, "what a nice girl!"

Little Fountain of Sakanoshita. 15

"Hum, tolerably," I answered with crafty dissimulation; but the cold corroboration was not received with composure.

"Why, she is a little beauty!" said my friend, with unnecessary emphasis.

"Yes, I suppose so," I remarked, continuing to dissemble, like the deep conspirator of a melodrama. "Where is my charioteer?" I added, addressing the new-comer, who still stood at the half-open door.

"Ah, Yamadori," she replied. "Does the gentleman want him?"

"So, Yamadori is his name. — I say, comrade, did you ever hear any thing like it? My *jin-riki-sha* fellow calls himself 'Mountain Bird,' and his sweetheart here is 'Little Fountain.'"

"Very appropriate."

"Well, Little Fountain, we do want Yamadori: we want him instantly."

"Extremely sorry, gentlemen; but he has gone back to Kameyama."

"What, gone back? Why, I must have him. Who is to take us on? Besides, he hasn't been paid."

"Oh! he spoke about the payment, and said, if the *danna* would give it to me to keep for him, it would be all the same. And, anyway, Yamadori could not go on with you. He takes travellers only from Sakanoshita to Kameyama and back."

"What nonsense! As to the payment, it is a trick; and he does not believe it will be the same. He thinks your smiling face will get him a double fare. Well, truly, I will not pay at all: I will pay nothing. I will even go and complain to the *nanushi*" (village magistrate).

The girl laughed merrily. "*Nanushi* knows what Yamadori is obliged to do." Then she grew preternaturally grave. "But, with regard to the trick, we are incapable of it."

"Of course, of course, Little Fountain! I am joking; but at the same time I am very angry. I like Yamadori, though I did not know his name; and I wanted him to show me every thing about this valley to-day. 'Tis a pity he did not speak to me about going."

"'Tis a pity the gentleman did not speak to him about staying. A traveller wished to start this morning at sunrise, — not a wealthy traveller and high officer like you, but nevertheless — And I am glad you like Yamadori. Everybody likes him."

"Except Little Fountain," I suggested.

"Except me, certainly. But he will be back to-night."

Little Fountain of Sakanoshita. 17

"Oh! will he?—I say, comrade, do you hear that? He will be back to-night."

"And we shall be in Kioto, I hope," replied my ambitious friend.

How long and how earnestly I labored to dissuade him from pursuing the journey with such violent haste, I need not here recount. He did not mind a day, he declared, provided it was to be devoted to a purpose; but here was a proposition to surrender twenty-four valuable hours to utter idleness, with the prospect of an equal delay to follow. It would not do: his mind was made up. For my own part, I was as fully resolved to linger. In the first place, I had been scorched so long on the To Kai Do, that I wanted a day or two of shady rest. In the next, I wanted to see more of this charming valley, which was unquestionably the most beautiful spot I had encountered, even in Japan. In the third, I wanted to confer upon a particular subject with Yamadori. I had always a passion for picking up good-looking servants in various parts of the land, and I meditated luring this brisk mountaineer to my distant home in Tokio. Lastly, there was that about Koïzumi which promised innocent entertainment, as well as opportunity for acquiring facility in the dialect of the old provinces, which I suddenly discovered was essential to the complete enjoyment of a visit to the ancient capital of the realm.

So we parted cordially; I promising to push on to Kioto within three days, — a promise, which, as I had no purpose of keeping it when I made it, there could be no possible wrong in breaking. At nine o'clock I was left alone, so far as the society of my own countrymen was concerned, in the heart of Japan. And alone I remained, I may as well here give notice, for seventeen consecutive days.

II.

As the morning advanced, I took measures to establish confidential relations with the members of the family, with the view of making myself as familiar as might be with the surroundings. From the beginning, Koïzumi was of infinite service to me. She was solicitous for my comfort, and expressed concern lest I should be disturbed by fleas. I admitted that their presence had already become more than a matter of suspicion on my part; whereupon, in a burst of candor, she declared her satisfaction that I had not questioned her on that point the evening before; "because, of course, I should have had to say there were no such things connected with our house." When pressed to disclose why the necessity for deception had existed then and disappeared to-day, she said it was now evident I had determined to remain a while: so it was useless to disguise the truth any longer. But I was not to suppose that they were very prevalent, or that carelessness was the cause of their coming: they *would* begin to thrive when houses grew old, and chambers went long unoccupied. "And we have very few visitors now," she added with a sigh. In fact, I soon learned that no stranger had stopped more than a single night, either at this house or any in the hamlet, for many months past.

While I gathered in all this and other information, I was carefully recording in my mind the various details of the little maid's personal appearance, and greatly regretting that I had no mastery of the pencil to fix the recollection more worthily and surely. There was no exaggeration in my friend's eulogiums. She *was* a little beauty; though why he said "little," and why I echo him, I am not altogether sure. Little for a Japanese, she probably was not. I should say her height was about five feet. In fact, not to deceive anybody, I happen to know it was exactly five feet; and that is considerably above the feminine average in the East. But we six-footed foreigners get easily in the way of applying diminutives to the gentle daughters of this land, and I have not yet heard that they are offended at it. Koïzumi was five feet tall, with a lithe and slender figure; and, being a working-girl, although the "daughter of the house," had a freedom and a grace of movement which the "quality" do not always possess, — chiefly, I think, because of their wrapping themselves so tightly all the while in their close-clinging robes. Naturally, there are no figures more perfect than those of the Japanese young women. The children up to the age of fourteen, or as long as they have the free use of their limbs, are models of symmetry. About that time they begin to fasten long garments about their hips, the effect of which is to impede their gait, and give them an awkward shamble. In course of time it does worse, and interrupts the development of their legs and thighs. Among the laboring class an additional misshapening is accomplished by the practice of carrying burdens, from an early age, upon the back, for the support of which broad straps are passed over the shoulders, and crossed in front, pressing directly upon the breasts. When a Japanese girl reaches the age of sixteen without having undergone either of these processes of deformity, she is a wonder to the eye, and remains so until twenty-five, or possibly a little later; then she ceases to charm, for a certain period, in any way excepting by her manner, and that is generally preserved to the last. But as she grows old, she has a chance of becoming quite delightful again. There is nothing nicer than a dignified and white-haired old Japanese lady. She is always happy, for she is always much respected and cherished by her youngers; and at a certain age the natural high-breeding of the race appears in her to attain its crystallization. Whatever her station in life, she is almost always sure to suggest an idea of ancient nobility, and to be surrounded by the atmosphere of an Oriental Faubourg St. Germain.

My heroine's middle position in life, at once relieving her from heavy drudgery, and emancipating her from the perpetual constraint of fashionable dress, was thus favorable to her aspect, viewing her from our settled standpoint. I have no doubt, that, if her own secret convictions could have been detected, they would have been found unflattering, at least to the extent of believing that her freedom from the pinched and contracted gait of the majority of her countrywomen was a disadvantage, and not a charm. Of course, we are all aware that no similar caprices of taste ever reveal themselves in the Western world. Koïzumi's private griefs, however, if she had any on the subject, did not concern me. Her possible fancies could be overlooked so long as she herself remained so agreeable a fact. As to her countenance, it was of the best Japanese type, — that type which defies ethnologists, and outfaces the Mongolian theory with noiseless but con-

Little Fountain of Sakanoshita. 23

vincing argument. Her complexion, though dark, was luminously clear; eyes round and flashing in animation, drooping and "long-drawn out" in quietude; firm but sweet-tempered mouth, with teeth within, the thought of whose chance future blackening made one thrill with horror; nose not too severe in regularity, and somewhat resolute chin; dimples *ad libitum*, by way of relief to any passing shade of sternness; face of exact oval shape, set off by piquant little ears, the lobes of which did not detach themselves, as those of our race generally do, from the cheek; the whole, of course, surmounted by a combination of the capillary fantasies of her nation, and presenting altogether such a picture as I hope, to put it with extreme mildness and moderation, I may live to see again.

Having extracted in a short time a large amount of local information from my quick-tongued little hostess (she was as voluble as she was vivacious in all other respects), I sauntered abroad to make practical use of it. But in this I was not altogether successful. The villagers overflowed with politeness, but were too much occupied with their usual avocations to go far out of their way to serve me. The children made the conventional pretence of timidity, and perhaps really felt it in this case, the sight of a foreigner being a remarkable, and to some of them an unprecedented, experience. So I presently found my way back to the Fuku-ya, where I set about inquiring, with some impatience, when my Mountain Bird would return to his roost. Koïzumi and her mother were very sorry, but he was not expected before the evening. As I showed signs of increasing dissatisfaction, I was requested to explain the particular duty I wished him to perform, as it might lie within their resources to supply a substitute. When I explained that what I needed was a guide to all the notable places of the neighborhood, the household brightened visibly; and Koïzumi *mère* hastened to assure me, that, although there really were no notable places about Sakanoshita, yet the whole locality was as familiar to all of them as to Master Yamadori. Singly or collectively they were at my disposal. Stay, she would go herself.

"But, *Oba-san* (aunty)," I interfered, "with your age and domestic responsibilities, I couldn't think of putting you to such inconvenience. Possibly some one of the young people, now"—

"To be sure: there are Takewo and Amegawa, and then here is my daughter; but she is a child, and might be troublesome."

On reflection, I concluded that the child would

not be troublesome, — not oppressively troublesome; and after a brief delay for *hiru-gohan* (the noon-meal), we started forth, Koïzumi enraptured at the prospect of exhibiting the beauties of her home, and I at once contented and expectant.

Undoubtedly she was a better pioneer than the Bird would have been; not only more agreeable, but practically better suited to my purpose. She was an enthusiast, full of sympathy, and, although she had always been a homekeeping maid, had any thing but homely wits. Suzuki Yama was the name of the mountain in the lap of which Sakanoshita[1] nestled; and before nightfall we knew most of its open roads, and a few of its more secluded pathways. When Yamadori came in with high-pressure speed and spirits, a little after sunset, he heard with intense satisfaction of the temporary engagement into which his sweetheart had entered, and, without being consulted, approved its indefinite extension. He entered voluntarily into a commercial statement of the case. If he remained at home to pilot me about the country, he could expect no better reward than that which he might otherwise gain in his normal pursuit; whereas the assumption

---

[1] Saka-no-shita: "Under the hillside," or "Beneath the slope."

of the charge by Koïzumi would prove an additional source of revenue, quite unlooked for, and tending to expedite connubial projects, the fulfilment of which was still undefined in the obscurity of the future. But, at this development of thrift, the matron became grave, and said that the honorable guest was entitled by every tradition of hospitality to the free command of all that she or hers could offer; and Koïzumi looked a little ashamed, and threw a reproachful glance at her swain, who, seeing that his speculative boldness had betrayed him into an indiscretion, went away, and hid himself for upwards of an hour.

It was, however, subsequently settled that the young man should continue to exercise his calling, and that Little Fountain should complete the work she had commenced, of instructing me in the geography of her district. Three days were sufficient to enable me to proceed on my explorations alone, with no danger of getting lost; and after that time I gave myself up to unrestrained mountain and forest revelry. It is a melancholy thing that words, at least such words as I can invoke, are so incompetent to reproduce the living beauty of this radiant Japanese scenery. There is nothing like it. I see no

Little Fountain of Sakanoshita. 27

opportunity of even a suggestion by comparison. One charm is its endless and often abrupt variety; another is its vivid and comprehensive clearness, due to the marvellous purity of the atmosphere. But what I find most winning of all is its quality of familiarness. No matter how infinite its wonders and glories, you may feel yourself on friendly terms with it from the first moment, and are never afterward repelled or dismayed by any sense of rigorous austerity. There is none of the cold severity which at times chills the generous influences of Switzerland. The gloom of bleak or barren grandeur is very rare; for the ruggedness of the mountain-tops is softened by verdure rising almost to the summits, — the desolation line being higher than in Europe or America. The character of the landscapes seems to be like that of the inhabitants. The valleys are always smiling to receive you, and the bamboo-crested hills are always nodding a welcome. I do not think it would be possible, for any length of time, to maintain perfectly easy relations with the Alps. Who would venture to take a liberty with Mont Blanc? But there is not a peak in all Japan with which you might not, at sight, exchange a good-natured jest, excepting, perhaps, Fuziyama, which, with all its feminine gentleness of demeanor, has a reputation for solemn majesty and haughty supremacy to sustain, and frowns upon frivolity or license.

Sakanoshita represents all that is most bewitching in Japanese life. It has no startling accessories, like the torrents at Nikkuo, — one of which plunges from a lofty lake over a precipice one-seventh of a mile in height, — and is guarded by no Vulcan's giants, like those which hover about Hakone; but it is crowded with natural fascinations, which, if not altogether so stately, are far more captivating. The people are Utopian; simple, affectionate, spirited, and ignorant rather than innocent of crime.[1] It was a pleasant fiction with them to pretend that the presence of a stranger added a new interest and vitality to existence in the valley, and it was a pleasant fact

[1] The chief magistrate was always eager to make me acquainted with the details of his office. I asked one day to see the district jail. "We have no jail," he said dejectedly, and seemed quite downcast at the absence of an institution which might have afforded me a moment's interest. "But what do you do with the people who misbehave, who steal, for example?" I asked. "Nobody ever steals," he replied, with a longer face than before, as if it had occurred to him for the first time that the existence of theft was an indispensable element in a finished state of society. What he said was perfectly true, and to this day it is true throughout the interior of Japan. In the open ports, where foreign customs are gradually making their way, this accessory of Western progress is to some extent understood.

Little Fountain of Sakanoshita. 29

with me to take it all for granted. Day after day passed along, the calmness of life diversified only by an occasional impatient note from my friend in advance, who, with every artifice of persuasion, endeavored to drag me forward. But I was too thoroughly at my ease to stir. Perfect contentment, for one unbroken week, was the prevailing sentiment of the little circle in which I moved, — I lazily, the *oba-san* maternally, Yamadori gallantly, and Koïzumi coquettishly contented; not a ripple on the surface of our satisfaction with ourselves and one another.

III.

AT the end of that period I fancied that I detected slight indications of change; nothing ominous, certainly not menacing, but still noteworthy to an observer of the fluctuations of rustic temper. They first exhibited themselves in a reluctance, on the *jin-riki-sha* runner's part, to undertake long journeys from home; unexpected returns at hours antedating those announced and agreed upon; a tendency to superfluous personal finery, wholly at variance with the economic principles of the head of the hostelry; and a fictitious exuberance of manner which contrasted disadvantageously with the previous accustomed spontaneity. Koïzumi's attention being called one day to these trifling phenomena, she assumed a droll expression, and withdrew to a corner conference with a cousin of her own sex and age; in which interchange of soul giggling predominated. It did not appear to concern me at all, nor should I have attached any significance to Master Yamadori's wavering moods, but for a circumstance that brought them directly under my attention.

Little Fountain of Sakanoshita. 31

Near the *yado-ya* was a fine little river in which I was accustomed to amuse myself every afternoon, stray villagers sometimes looking on, with no particular purpose, from a bridge above. On one occasion Koïzumi was among the spectators, and in the evening she greatly terrified me by proposing that I should teach her to swim.

I assured her that it would be altogether too difficult; that, in fact, it was impossible.

She could not understand that at all. "You can swim better than anybody," she was pleased to say.

"Undoubtedly," I answered. "But it is one thing to know how to swim, and another to know how to teach others to swim."

Koïzumi accused me of sophistry.

"And moreover," I urged, "I do not speak Japanese well enough, as you ought to be aware."

Koïzumi politely intimated that that was absurd, and added that it was immaterial to her whether she acquired the art of natation upon the Japanese or English system. She had few anti-foreign prejudices. There were no edicts against adopting Western science to that extent, at least; and mere bathing was not necessarily baptism.

"Here is Yamadori," said I: "he will teach you by and by, after you are married."

She tossed her pretty head. "When I want a thing, I want it immediately."

"Well, he will teach you any time you like, then, I suppose."

"Yes, certainly!" assented Yamadori with eagerness. "I will teach you immediately."

"That is nonsense, Yamadori. You do not know how to swim yourself."

"Koïzumi, it does not matter," he retorted. "I will learn to-morrow, or the next time I go to Kuwana. I will go on purpose."

But destiny decreed that the young enthusiast should not see Kuwana on the following day, nor for many days to come. He started at an early hour, with a "fare" for Kameyama, promising to return at three o'clock, by which I understood him to mean, from recent experience, a little after noon. On this occasion, however, he was better, or worse, than his word. I had been wandering in the afternoon with my pleasant companion, carefully avoiding all streams of suggestive magnitude, and came out toward sundown upon the main road, where, to the amazement of both of us, Yamadori presently appeared with a most dejected 'havior of the visage, entirely alone, dragging no wagon behind him.

"Why, my lad, what is the matter?"

Little Fountain of Sakanoshita. 33

"Where is the *kuruma* (vehicle)?" said Koïzumi, who, though on affection bent, had yet a frugal mind.

Yamadori sat down in the middle of the To Kai Do, resting his weight upon his heels, which is the common attitude of Japanese repose, and began to cry.

"Come," said I, "this will not do. Koïzumi, tell him to get up and speak."

She responded by sitting down likewise in the middle of the To Kai Do, upon her heels, and crying in obligato.

"Well," said I, much bewildered, "if there were only one of you going crazy, I might be successful in consoling. Under the circumstances I shall leave you to console each other."

This was because I felt convinced that something really serious must have happened, according to their measurement of seriousness, and that I should be doing them the best favor by ostensibly making light of the mysterious catastrophe, and giving them an opportunity for comforting communion. At the same time it made me very uneasy to see my favorites overcome by such an unusual excess of emotion. Except through the imagination, a Japanese is not easily moved to a display of grief. He will mourn over the sorrows of a hero of romance, and utterly dissolve before theatrical representations of human woe; but in the affairs of his own life he is apt to be a stoic.

I went back to the inn alone, and sat in the gateway, waiting for the return of the young couple. It was not long before they re-appeared, but they did not immediately enter the house. After a little low conversation outside, Koïzumi turned and came indoors alone; while Yamadori moved on toward the upper end of the village.

"Well, my child," said I, as she passed me, "if you can tell me what the matter is, pray do. Tell me whenever you like."

She looked anxiously at me, paused a moment, then shook her head, and went in out of sight.

Presently she re-appeared, and knelt down very submissively, — which, I should say, is a form of courtesy, and not of humiliation, — and said she hoped I would excuse her if she had been rude; but her heart was very heavy.

"Poor Little Fountain!" said I. "But, if you do not tell me what it is, how can I help you?"

"So I would willingly, and I wish to," she replied; "but Yamadori says I must not."

Of course, the instant I heard this, I became abnormally eager to know, and determined to use every effort to that end: so I hinted with sarcas-

Little Fountain of Sakanoshita. 35

tic bitterness, that, oh! if she thought I was not her friend, and if Yamadori was disposed to forestall his matrimonial authority to the extent of shutting her out from the sympathy of the world, and she was content to suffer such tyranny, there was nothing more to say, and I would go and pack my portmanteau at once; which was about as cruel a thing as I ever did in my life, and for which I was punished, as soon as I saw the piteous expression of her face, by a conviction of meanness that made me long to inflict upon myself the Japanese penalty to which Yamadori had been driven on the second night of my sojourn, and withdraw to inaccessible solitudes.

She looked at me intently for an instant, and then with a sigh said that I misunderstood her and also misunderstood him. But she could tell me a part of the misfortune; in fact, all about that. There was only a small something connected with it which she was forbidden to divulge. And then the worst of it came out. In hurrying to get back to Sakanoshita before his time, Yamadori had run too rapidly around a dangerous corner, had upset his *jin-riki-sha* over a rocky ledge, and broken it to irremediable smash.

"Is that all?" I asked composedly.

"All!" she cried; and her eyes actually opened

to that extent that they became oval in the wrong direction, that is, perpendicularly, — " all ! Is it not enough ? "

" But he was not hurt ? "

" Hurt ? No : he is not the man to cry because he is hurt. But the *jin-riki-sha*."

" Ah ! There was a passenger ? "

" I do not know. I believe so. I forget."

" And was he hurt ? "

" How should I know ? It is the *jin-riki-sha* that we are thinking of. Almost new ; it cost fifteen *riyos* at the beginning of the fifth month."

" I see," said I, endeavoring to enter into her view of the subject. " And he cannot buy another."

" Buy another ? *Oya, oya !* How could he ever buy *one?* Did you think it was his ? Oh, no, sir ! Yamadori is very poor : he has never had fifteen *riyos* in his life, — not all at once. All the *jin-riki-shas* in Sakanoshita belong to the merchant Sakurai, the wealthiest man of our town, the *nanushi*. Yamadori has gone now to tell him. What shall we do ? "

Gradually it dawned upon me that in a sequestered little community like this, where trade had hardly ever been known, where husbandmen wrung their subsistence from the soil with ceaseless labor, and where industry was of necessity so slightly rewarded that the daily wages of the most assiduous toiler could not exceed half a *bu*, or about twelve cents, an accident like this which had befallen the lad might be nothing less than a calamity. As I was turning this new phase of the business in my mind, and trying to fix upon some appropriate observation, I remarked casually and indifferently, and with no definite purpose of any kind, "What on earth made him run so fast?"

"Ah!" said Koïzumi, shrinking back, "that is what I am not to tell you."

It is extraordinary how a habit of despotism will grow upon us. I had been exercising unlimited sway over this establishment for several days, to my own complete satisfaction, and apparently to that of the inmates. Having been monarch of all I surveyed, I resented the idea that there should be any my right to dispute. So, although it is not exactly pleasant to confess it, I drew into my shell again. I made no further allusion to portmanteaus, not having the pluck to risk a second reproachful gaze from those great sorrowful eyes; but I said with considerable asperity of tone, "Why, Koïzumi, will you not tell me?"

"I cannot. He would be angry."

"Who, Master Yamadori? I should like to see him angry with me!"

"No, no; not with you, but with me. He would only be ashamed with you."

"Why should he be ashamed, then?"

"But that is what I must not say."

"Listen to me, Koïzumi. I really want to know."

"Truly I cannot."

"Listen to me, I say" —

"I will ask him, and if he permits me" —

"If you will not listen to me, there is an end to every thing. Never mind about asking him. Tell me all about it before he returns, because I want to think of some plan by which you shall be able to make it all right for him without any delay."

"It is very kind; and I thank you. But I cannot."

"As you please," said I in dudgeon, and walked out of the gate, and began to climb the hill. I suppose I was firmly convinced, at the time, that my urgency was solely in my little friend's interest, and that I alone was aggrieved by her dauntlessness, while she suffered nothing from my persistence.

The *nanushi* lived at the upper end of the

Little Fountain of Sakanoshita. 39

village ; and, as I drew near his house, Yamadori issued forth, still in deep discomfiture. He looked shyly at me, and seemed disposed to avoid my side of the road. Being still huffily inclined, I made no effort to check his homeward progress. Influenced by a new idea, however, I walked straight to the *nanushi's* door, and, summoning a servant, sent in a message requesting an interview. In an instant the worthy elder was on the threshold, profusely hospitable and polite, and proposing tea and biscuit with an eagerness that would not be denied. This exactly suited my sudden purpose. A moment later I was seated in the midst of his abundant family, exchanging broadsides of compliment with the entire group.

After this inevitable prelude, I proceeded to the object of my call. The *nanushi* was good enough to give me the freest information concerning the matter in hand. The *jin-riki-sha* business was not without its hazards, as Yamadori's mishap had proved. An operator, even upon so humble a scale as his own, ran serious risks. By careful management he had accumulated four of these costly vehicles during the past six months ; and now one of them, the most recent of the lot, had been sacrificed. Of course it was not the boy's fault ; he knew that, and was not disposed to be hard upon him; but what could he do? One-fourth of his wheeled capital destroyed by carelessness: at least he supposed it must be carelessness, for he could not get any satisfactory explanation of the cause of Yamadori's excessive haste. Yes, he had *kagos* — a dozen of them; but *kagos* were used now only for crossing the mountain toward Lake Biwa. Nobody would think of using them on level ground in this age of progress. It would cost him two months' profits to get another *kuruma*, for people were mistaken in supposing him to be a man of superfluous means: he was only prosperous according to a village standard. And, even when he should get one, could he venture to confide it to a young man who had that day shown himself unworthy of so grave a responsibility?

I asked if Yamadori had ever before been found wanting.

"That he has not," interposed a brisk young lady of twenty, who sat in a corner. "He is the best boy in the province."

"My daughter is forward," said the *nanushi;* "but, making certain allowances, she is just. Yamadori has hitherto been above reproach."

"And he is very popular and swift," added the young girl, "and brings in as much money as any two of the others."

Little Fountain of Sakanoshita. 41

"I was about to say so," remarked her father, "in language not less convincing, though possibly less violent."

"I should think then, Master *Nanushi*, that you might venture to stand by him again."

"Since the gentleman is good enough to be interested in him, I would willingly do so; but I cannot afford to purchase another *jin-riki-sha* within less than two months, and certainly I cannot dismiss one of my men who has done no wrong, to accommodate another who at least has been awkward and unskilful."

"Meanwhile he may starve," said the impetuous advocate in the corner.

"Nobody starves in Sakanoshita!" said the *nanushi* severely. "Such a thing would be a sorrow to the people: it has never been heard of, and never will be."

I began to fear that the energetic young lady would injure my cause, but felt grateful nevertheless for her support. "Can nothing be done?" I asked, after a minute's pause.

"I might put him upon a *kago*," said the old man, reflectively.

"A *kago*, and give him a hump!" exclaimed the daughter.

"A hump on the shoulder is better than emptiness in the belly," said the worthy magistrate: "I can do no better. I wish I could; for I like the lad, as everybody does."

"I am obliged to you, Master *Nanushi*, and especially obliged to your amiable daughter. Yamadori will be pleased to learn that he has had so charming and effective an advocate."

The young lady came forward to the light, and revealed a countenance the gratification in which was unmistakable. I was pleased at having produced an agreeable effect, and determined to improve it. "And Koïzumi, too, will be very thankful," I added. But this, alas! was a failure, an unquestionable anti-climax. The young lady's face grew as long as one of her own sleeves, and her brow as dark as the obscurity from which she had emerged. "I suppose the *kagos* are too good for him, after all," she remarked, and turned away pettishly. In taking the last extra step I had clearly put my foot in it. Nothing, however, could be gained by prolonging the conversation; and, observing that I was glad to have the *nanushi's* promise, I formally withdrew, wondering a little, but not much, at the daughter's variable temper.

IV.

THEY keep early hours in Sakanoshita. I saw nobody but a servant when I returned to the Fuku-ya, and heard nothing of the absorbing topic until next morning, when, as I was dressing, Yamadori presented himself, and begged to know if I could listen to him for a few minutes. I told him I should be very glad; and he came in, but was even more embarrassed than he had previously appeared. After several false starts, he began, with many halts and hitches, to say that Koïzumi had told him I wished to know the reason of his ruinous haste the day before; and that, though suffering from profound mortification, he was prepared to inform me. I instantly became unreasonable and autocratic again. "I do not wish to hear it," said I, "except from Koïzumi herself: she offended me by refusing to tell me yesterday, and I cannot suffer any such evasion as this." To my surprise, the lad seemed much relieved, and went hastily away to report my determination.

I did not see the little delinquent, as I chose

to stigmatize her, for an hour or more. At last she came, looking prettily penitent, and declared herself ready to submit to my commands in all things. Whereupon, like most despots under similar circumstances, I became extremely gracious, called for tea and jelly, and invited her to be as confidential as she pleased.

"Now that Yamadori has consented," she began, "I am ready enough. But it is a very little thing. He would much rather have me tell than be obliged to do it himself. You may laugh at him; but I hope you will not be angry."

"Very good, Koïzumi: for your sake I will not be angry."

"And, after all, I am the one that is really to blame."

"As to that, Koïzumi, we shall see."

"The truth is" — (Giggle.)

"Well?"

"He was hurrying home" — (Many giggles.)

"Go on."

"Because he was afraid you would be teaching me to swim." (Countless giggles.)

"Bless us!"

"Yes. And what is more, he is" —

"What?"

"Jealous, and has been for several days."

Little Fountain of Sakanoshita. 45

"Koïzumi, this is very dreadful."

"Is it, indeed? I know little about such things. But I hope you are not angry."

"No, Koïzumi, I am not, — that is, not exactly angry, — certainly not with you, nor yet with Yamadori. But, — on the whole, you are a good and faithful little girl. I have a great regard for you. Your obedience to your betrothed is extremely praiseworthy. I should have liked it just as well if you had not told me at all."

"But, dear sir, you insisted."

"So I did. And what is to be done now, I wonder?"

"Well, there is something else to be said, and this is indeed difficult. The other was nothing — it was only Yamadori's fancy; but now, truly, I am almost in despair."

"Koïzumi," said I, "it does not appear that the result of my endeavors to force you to betray confidence has been eminently happy. If your betrothed has again forbidden you" —

"Yes, he has forbidden me."

"Then say no more. I excuse you."

"He has forbidden me, but that is nothing."

"You amaze me. How can it be nothing to-day, when yesterday it was every thing?"

"Gentle sir, it is wholly a different matter.

To begin with, a great deal of time has passed since yesterday. Next, Yamadori then forbade me on his own account; he thought you would never forgive him; whereas now he forbids me on my own account, because it is entirely my own affair. Finally, if I can get courage to speak at all, I do not propose to trouble myself about Yamadori's permission."

The rural simplicity of Sakanoshita maidenhood was evidently getting beyond my sphere of comprehension. I prudently said nothing.

"You know, sir," said Koïzumi, — and there could be no doubt about the sincerity of her anxiety this time, — "that the *nanushi* is very rich. I must tell you, also, that he has an itching palm.[1] He is doubtless irritated at the loss of his property, and Yamadori is sure to be dismissed from his employment. But the *nanushi* has a great respect for treasure and station. Now, I have had a thought, that if a noble officer in the service of the government, and one of such wealth that figures cannot measure it, would consent to intercede for him, the stern magistrate and merchant would be merciful. O dear sir!

[1] Lest any should suspect me of embellishing the vernacular, let me observe that "an itching palm" is a common Japanese figure of speech; not the only one, by scores, that is identical with familiar idioms of Western tongues.

pray do this for poor Yamadori, and forgive the presumption of the rude girl who trembles while she asks it."

"Little Fountain," said I, "you are a good girl. I said so before, and I see no reason to alter my judgment. But I understand that rank and riches are needed to exercise the influence you speak of. Now, the truth is, that I have neither."

"O sir! Yamadori told me" —

"That I had one thousand *riyos* a month. I know he did; but it is not true. He is a fine romancer. Here, I will show you my passport; you shall know all about it."[1]

"It is not necessary, since you tell me so. But what does it matter? Yamadori has told everybody the same, and the whole village thinks it is true."

It appeared, then, that I was not to attribute my influence with the *nanushi* wholly to my power of personal persuasion. Perhaps it was all the better: any way, I could offer some reparation

---

[1] For what earthly purpose they do it I cannot say; but, in granting travelling passports to an employee, the officers of the government insist upon introducing all possible particulars of his private life, — his age, birthplace, occupation, and even the exact amount of his salary. Yamadori had heard this sum named at some of the stations where my permit had been examined, and, for reasons before mentioned, had magnified it out of all reason.

for my bad treatment of the young girl, if that were really all she wanted of me.

"And this is all, Koïzumi, that you have to ask?"

"That is all: I am only afraid it is too much."

"You are quite sure there is nothing else you wish me to do?"

"Why, what else can there be?" she asked with genuine perplexity.

"What else, to be sure?" said I, dismissing my suspicions. "Very good, my dear: you may set your mind at rest."

"You will do it?"

"I have done it. I saw the *nanushi* last night."

The grateful little thing tried to laugh, and not to cry, and failed in both efforts. "O Yamadori!" she screamed, "come here and thank the gentleman, for I have no words to do it."

Yamadori was not far distant,—not beyond her call. He came slowly and sheepishly, and, in consequence of an hysterical incoherence into which his sweetheart immediately fell, remained insensible for a while to the brightened prospect of his situation. When at last it broke upon him, he was much moved, but only said, " I am sure that the gentleman would not have done this for me if he had not forgiven me for my folly."

Little Fountain of Sakanoshita. 49

"And me for mine," said Koïzumi.

As it was distinctly obvious that the girl had done nothing but exactly what was best all through, this seemed an illogical proposition. But she was determined to be pardoned jointly with her swain, and laid so much stress upon it, that there was no escape, and I was compelled to pronounce a solemn absolution in the approved style of the ancient and honorable English comedies.

For the remainder of the morning I abandoned myself to revery. A few additional words had shown me that Yamadori was ready enough to accept the inferior occupation of *kago*-bearer; though Koïzumi, like the magistrate's daughter, was troubled about his shoulders, and promised to make him a nice soft pad. I began to ask myself the question why — although I was not a high officer with one thousand monthly *riyos* — I could not go out of my way to practically smooth the difficult course of this village love. I certainly felt deeply interested in the young people. But, if that circumstance were to stand as sufficient justification, there would be nothing to hinder me from going about, and proffering material assistance to thirty-three millions of people, that being the aggregate population of Japan according to the last government census. It is rather a peril-ous precedent, to give way to one's impulses of profusion in this country, the temptations are so frequent and powerful. For nearly two hours I reflected, and then announced a journey. Two of the *nanushi's* ablest *jin-riki-sha* men should that afternoon convey me to Kameyama, fifteen miles distant. where I could pass the night, and return the next day at my convenience.

This was sufficient to constitute an event in our circle; and you may be sure that I threw as much mystery about it as I could, expressly to heighten expectation. I admitted that I had a project, and an important one, but declared that nobody should know what it was, or whom it concerned, until my own time of disclosure. Yamadori regretted that he should not have the privilege of assisting in drawing me; and Koïzumi begged me not to remain too long away, lest the *nanushi* should extricate himself from the spell of my influence, and retract his promises. I played Alexander, affected to nod, and intimated, that, as I had taken the affairs of the universe under my control, no person need concern himself as to the results. That night I slept at Kameyama.

The next morning, having paid my runners, and notified them that they need not wait to take me back, I visited the quarter of the carpenters and

Little Fountain of Sakanoshita. 51

wagon-manufacturers. This town is not without a reputation for the neat and substantial vehicles it produces; and, after a little search, I found a capital double *jin-riki-sha*,— firm, compact, not too heavy, and refulgent with red lacquer. Half an hour of tolerably tough bargaining put it in my possession at a reasonable sum. Long before noon I was on my way to the mountains again, this time propelled by strangers. Our arrival in front of the Fuku-ya created a sensation. Yamadori was up on the hill, at the *kago* depot; but he soon came running down to learn the cause of my strange action in sending home the other *kuruma* without an occupant.

" We were afraid you meant to remain away a long time," said Little Fountain.

" Some of us thought you were dissatisfied with the way in which the *jin-riki-sha* was managed," said Yamadori.

" The *jin-riki-sha* was well enough pulled, although your hand was wanting, my lad. But the weather was warm and uncomfortable, and I fancied a larger one to come home in : so you see " —

" Truly, that is a majestic piece of work," he replied, inspecting the new vehicle with the appreciative eye of a connoisseur.

' Do you like it? " said I.

He examined it closely before answering. "I have conceived a better one," he finally remarked; "but I never saw one so good. Perhaps there are none finer in Tokio?" he added inquiringly.

"I am glad you like it," said I; "for it is yours, Yamadori." And I precipitately retired from mortal view, in imitation of a certain effect I had often admired in melodramas.

For several minutes I was allowed to be alone. Then the daughter of the house peeped into my room, and regarded me silently with an expression that confused me not a little.

"Come," I exclaimed, "say something, you stupid girl!"

"I understand well that the gentleman does not wish to hear too many thanks," she answered; "and I could not talk about any thing else. Koïzumi's heart is very full."

"Nonsense, you silly child! and all about a two-wheeled cart. What does your sweetheart say?"

"Oh! Yamadori — he is crazy with delight and fear."

"Why with fear?"

"He thinks that the *nanushi* may make a claim on the *kuruma*, or its earnings, in return for that which he lost."

Little Fountain of Sakanoshita. 53

"I do not think that will be possible, unless it was in his agreement that he should make good all accidental losses. But it can be easily arranged. I can give the new *jin-riki-sha* to you, my dear; and you, I suppose, will not refuse to lend it to him, if he behaves himself."

So that little business was comfortably settled; the *nanushi*, moreover, declaring that nothing would be further from his designs than to interfere harshly with the young man's unexpected prosperity; only, as he had shown himself generously disposed when his good-will had seemed important, he thought that Yamadori ought to take a new proposal from him into favorable consideration; and this was nothing more nor less than that, instead of attempting an injudicious rivalry in so small a field, they should unite their capital, and form a *kuruma* partnership, Yamadori's acquisition, together with his strength and agility, to entitle him to two-fifths of the profits of the business, and he to pay three-fifths of the cost of the next *jin-riki-sha* purchased on joint account. I thought so too, and said to Koïzumi that I imagined her view of the old gentleman's character had been hasty, and that, if his palm itched at all, it was to perform deeds of benevolence, and nothing more. But she did not take very kindly to the alliance, though she would not oppose it. As to Yamadori, he thought it was the most superb opening that could be dreamed of. The affair, I considered, was virtually accomplished, and, precisely as it had been a week before, beatitude seemed to reign universal and supreme.

V.

WE know what often happens to the best laid schemes of all animals, low and high. In less than forty-eight hours, portentous signs began to manifest themselves, this time from a novel quarter, which presently assumed a highly ominous form. It was no other than Koïzumi who now departed from the even current of her usual placidity. She ceased to smile, was petulant without apparent cause, and once or twice was bitter in repartee. In consequence of which it became proper for me to interfere again.

"Koïzumi, come hither: you are in new trouble."

"I? Not at all. I care nothing, however much he may misbehave."

"So, Yamadori is in mischief once more. Tell me, is he jealous still?"

"Sir, he was never jealous. It was a deception. How could he be jealous when he has cared nothing for me all the while?"

It was more and more evident that I must have a finger in the pie. "I am determined that you children shall not make yourselves miserable," I declared. "Let me know at once what has happened."

"In this case, sir," she said, sitting down beside me, "there is no remedy. Yamadori has deserted me."

"Deserted you? Impossible. He was here this morning."

"Oh! he continues to come; but he has deserted me, all the same. We have quarrelled desperately."

"It must be a capital sight to see you try to quarrel, Koïzumi."

"I can do it if I wish. I have called him such names!—but nothing like what he deserves. If you would only teach me how to talk to him in English."

"To swear at him, I suppose you mean."

"To swear at him, yes."[1]

"Koïzumi, I will undertake that task, if it is really necessary. Now, explain every thing."

Gradually I made myself master of the facts. They did not look well for Yamadori. He had shown himself fickle. Either his heart was not

[1] It is impossible to be profane in Japanese. The language contains nothing in the way of violence. The strongest terms of objurgation are "fool" and "beast;" and they are very rarely heard, except from the lips of foreigners.

Little Fountain of Sakanoshita. 57

constant, or the new *jin-riki-sha* had got into his head. I found that the *nanushi's* daughter, who had interested herself so warmly in his behalf, had for a long time been suspected of a hidden partiality for him, which it would have been hopeless to openly display; but that, since the young man had suddenly become a capitalist, she had felt free to hang out signals that could not be mistaken by the slowest of perceptions. The father had not shown himself averse, and Yamadori was rapidly giving way to the flattering influence. My little girl was quite convinced that her lover was as good as lost.

"This is incredible," said I, "it is monstrous. I have seen her. She is not nearly so pretty as you, and I am sure she cannot be so accomplished."

"It may be so, sir; but I think that you foreigners place more value upon good looks than we do. Nobody ever said much about mine before you came here; and accomplishments go for little when they are not joined to wealth."

"But you, Koïzumi, should be a person of distinction. You are the daughter of the first *yado-ya* in Sakanoshita, and you will one day be the mistress of it. That is a position. Why, the *nanushi's* house is not half so large as yours."

"That is nothing, now. I have heard that when the great *daimios* used to pass through, in former years, we were well to do. I can just remember those days. We had twenty servants then. It is very different now, as any one may see."

"He is blind, he is an idiot."

"No, he is not an idiot; but he is *date-sha*, and his vanity is the strongest part of him. He cannot resist the temptation to make himself the first man of the village."

"I will speak to him, directly."

"That would never do. I am very fond of him; but I could not be happy if he were forced to return to me against his will. No, sir, you are very kind, and I am wretched; but you must not try to help me in this."

"What is to be done, then?"

"I will think about it all the afternoon. I will go to Inari-sama,[1] and perhaps something will come to me."

Koïzumi's complaint was easily verified, and that without any direct questioning. Strolling forth, I found the inconstant at the *jin-riki-sha* house, inspecting the stock, oiling, polishing, and

---

[1] Inari-sama is the fox deity, whose temples are in high esteem among young lovers.

repairing here and there, and chatting at intervals with his aged partner's daughter, who was continually " happening in " from the dwelling-house, on the most transparently fictitious errands. The minx had actually the effrontery to thank me for my present to Yamadori, who heard her without being abashed in the smallest degree; at which, fearing to derange Koïzumi's plans — if she should form any — by a premature explosion, I walked away in silent indignation.

Returning to the inn, I found the maiden I had left forlorn in the hands of the barber, who was erecting a marvellous structure upon her head. She had a *samisen* on her knee, and was practising jubilant melodies. Here was a new surprise. Had the wind changed again?

" I have an idea," whispered Koïzumi, getting up, and following me. " Inari-sama has inspired me. I hope it will do; and I am sure it will, if you will help me."

" I will do any thing you like."

" Mountains of thanks. Yamadori will be here this evening, as usual; or, if he is not, I shall send for him. I shall have many things to say to him, most of which will not be true; but that makes little difference."

" The end justifies the means," said I.

"I don't understand that," said Koïzumi; "but I shall tell a great many fibs, all of which came to me this afternoon at the temple. What I wish to ask is, that you will not contradict any thing I may say."

"Very good. I will contradict nothing."

"And you will support me if necessary?"

"Ah! that is serious; and I am in the dark."

"Oh, there shall be no harm! Inari-sama is responsible." And she laughed merrily, as if confident, in anticipation, of success.

"I suppose I must trust Inari-sama for the sake of his disciple," said I.

"My mother approves, and will also assist me."

"Good. You make me very curious."

"By and by, sir, you shall see and hear every thing. To tell you now would spoil all."

At seven o'clock in the evening I was requested to visit that part of the house in which the head of the family resided, where I found a considerable gathering of neighbors, seated in a hollow square, with little boxes of refreshments before them. They bent forward to salute me as I entered, and then silently resumed their tea and pipes. This was obviously a ceremonial re-union of some significance. For a moment I thought

Little Fountain of Sakanoshita. 61

that a reconciliation had taken place, and that I had been summoned to assist at the nuptial party. But the fact that Yamadori was not present invalidated this conjecture. Inasmuch as I knew nothing, and yet was expected, according to Koïzumi, to appear to know every thing, I maintained a discreet silence. An elderly lady volunteered a recitative, and a younger one vouchsafed a dance; at the end of which the truant stalked in, not a little overcome by the unaccustomed brilliancy of the scene. He understood it more readily than I.

"Why, this is a farewell," he said. "Who is going away?" And, answering himself, "It must be the noble gentleman. Truly this is a sorrow to Sakanoshita."

Koïzumi, who was tightening the strings of a *samisen* as he entered, here interrupted him with a merry song, then popular all over Japan, the refrain of which was "*Jin-riki-sha abunai*" ('ware *jin-riki-sha*), in the selection of which I detected mischief. Having finished, she turned to Yamadori, and said in her most musical tones, "Yes, we are going, and within two days. We are very glad you have come."

"'We'! *Domo, domo!* May I ask who are 'we'?"

"The *danna-san* and myself," said Koïzumi, gayly and unblushingly.

Yamadori let fall an exclamation of astonishment in ten syllables, while I rose to remonstrate. But a quick glance from the principal actress in the comedy reminded me that I had pledged myself to acquiescence in all that she might aver. Certainly I had not bargained for this sort of thing; but I was bound not to hazard the success of my heroine's plot, whatever it might be, to say nothing of the personal interest I felt in its development.

"The gentleman has decided to increase the number of his servants at Tokio, which his magnificent income of one thousand *riyos* a month enables him to do without limit. He is so good as to say that nobody else in the empire can put on buttons or repair his wardrobe as well as I can. Therefore we proceed at once to Kioto, stopping one day at Lake Biwa in order that he may teach me to swim."

"Is this really true?" faltered Yamadori.

"*Sayo de gozarimasu,*" corroborated the assemblage.

"And is your mother going with you?"

"Foolish boy! Who would take care of the *yado-ya?* Besides which, she has no desire to travel, and is too old to learn to swim. Sit down, Yamadori."

He collapsed in a daze, looked stupidly around, and sighed heavily.

"You ought to be very glad," said an old gossip: "it will be a great relief to you."

Yamadori looked fiercely at her, said nothing, but swallowed cups of hot tea with rapidity.

"And now, Yamadori," continued the young girl, with such singular sweetness that I made sure a *coup de grâce* was coming, "we shall be sorry to incommode you; but I shall naturally require my *jin-riki-sha*. If you will bring it to-morrow, I shall be obliged."

"Your *jin-riki-sha?*"

"Yes, the new one."

Yamadori started to his feet. "Why, it is mine!" he exclaimed. "I am going to add it to the *nanushi's* lot, and we are to do business together."

"Oh, no, my friend!" said Koïzumi in softer and more melodious accents than I had ever heard from her lips. "It is mine, and was given to me. I only promised to lend it to you when I found it convenient. My generous benefactor and master remembers."

"To be sure I remember," said I, glad to be

able to support her truthfully in one statement.

Yamadori stood motionless and very pale for a moment. "I have been a brute," at last he murmured: "now I am properly rewarded." And he turned away trembling, and departed without saying good-night.

Then came Koïzumi's hardest trial. She was obliged to remain hours later, and keep up the semblance of festivity, for the numerous guests had no conception of the unreality of the scene in which they were taking part. She had confided in nobody but her mother.

After it was all over, she came, wearily and timidly, and asked if I thought it would succeed.

"If it does not, young woman," said I, " you have put me into a pretty position. You may well say that you got the idea from Inari. You are a fox yourself."

"Of course, sir, I have taken a great liberty. But truly, I was desperate: I am so fond of him! I was convinced you would not consent if I told you my plan beforehand, and so" —

"You played Inari with me."

"Forgive me."

"Oh! I don't care, if it does not fail."

"It will not fail: it has succeeded already."

Little Fountain of Sakanoshita. 65

"How can you know that?"

"Inari tells me so."

It did not take long, the following morning, for us to arrange the closing act of the drama. Yamadori came about ten o'clock, and deposited the vehicle which had been his delusion and destruction before the gate. His expression was not one of penitence: he seemed to have fallen beyond that, into complete hopelessness. But it was not my cue to relieve him too suddenly.

"Your *jin-riki-sha* is here, Koïzumi," he said. "You will find it no worse than when I took it. I should have brought it earlier; but I had to look at the springs, and oil the wheels, and put on a new nut at this side."

"That is very thoughtful of you," said I.

He saluted me gravely, but made me no answer.

"I hear you are going to-morrow," he resumed, turning to Koïzumi.

"I believe so," she answered. "The *kami-san* (lady of the house) will be happy to see you whenever you choose to come; but I suppose you will amuse yourself best with your friends at the *nanushi's*."

"I do not think the *nanushi* would receive me now; and, if he would, I should not go there.

Nobody in Sakanoshita will ever see me after you depart."

"What do you mean, Yamadori? and where will you go?"

"It does not matter, and I do not know; but I cannot stay in this place."

"Yamadori, I hope you do not think I have treated you ill."

"You, Koïzumi! you have never shown me any thing but kindness."

"Look here, my lad," I put in, "since you are going to quit this place, why not come along with us? or, if you wish, you can take any road you like best, and meet us at the Eastern Capital. My house is large enough, and I am always getting new servants."

"I see that the gentleman is always getting new servants," said Yamadori, still overlooking me, and addressing Koïzumi; "though, by the by, I told you a falsehood when I said his income was a thousand *riyos*. Never mind. He is very good, but I cannot go with him to Tokio."

"Come, Yamadori," said I, relenting a little before the stipulated time (for, although he had undoubtedly behaved badly, he was suffering torments for it, and in his last new attitude he was manly and honorable), "I believe, after all, that

Little Fountain of Sakanoshita. 67

you cannot bear to part from Koïzumi. Perhaps she is willing enough not to part from you; but when you began it, which you certainly did, she was perfectly free to look out for herself. Now you seem to take it greatly to heart: if she is willing to have compassion on you, I will not be hard. She may stay if she chooses, and our contract shall be void. But I make two conditions: you must marry her immediately, and the *jinriki-sha* and any other things I may give her must be hers forever. I leave you to decide the matter between you." And then I hurried away, knowing well that it was already decided in both their minds before I had finished speaking.

That night there was another feast at the Fukuya,—a genuine wedding jubilee. Almost all Sakanoshita was there, even the *nanushi*. His eldest daughter was prevented from attending by a trifling indisposition. In the midst of the proceedings Koïzumi made opportunity for a few words with me.

"I do not know when I shall venture to tell him the truth," said she; "probably never. But I do think, that, after it is all over, I may safely say that the *kuruma* shall be his."

"You are a foolish little girl," said I; "but you shall do as you please."

VI.

It was time for me to close my holidays among the mountains. The long vacation was nearly over, and I had yet the old metropolis to see. Two days later I started westward. Koïzumi gave me a little wallet, which she had worked with her own hands, and which I use to this day. She regretted that her poverty prevented her from offering a worthier gift; but she could not have thought of any thing prettier or more serviceable. Yamadori bestowed upon me one of the ingenious paper lanterns of that district, which can be folded, and carried in the pocket. He testified his devotion in two other ways: first, on the back of the *jin-riki-sha* he painted my monogram in brilliant colors, copied from an envelope which Koïzumi picked out of a packet for him, and, alluding to it as my "crest" (*mon*), vowed that it should always shine there in remembrance of me; next, although wholly unused to the work, he insisted on bearing one end of the pole of the *kago* in which I was carried toward Ootsu

I promised that I would certainly return to Sakanoshita during the next semi-annual recess, and I meant to do so when I said it. But something else turned up, as it always happens, and I suppose it is a question if I ever see the place or them again. Once in a great while I receive little scraps of letters from them. They say that they are happy, and do not forget me.

TO FUZIYAMA AND BACK.

I.

FUZIYAMA, the loftiest and most celebrated peak of Japan, can be ascended with comfort, I may even say with safety, only in the months of July and August, and occasionally in the early part of September. At all other times its summit is covered with snow. When, therefore, a few days after my arrival in that land, which was at the end of a certain August, the suggestion broke forth one evening, that a compact and sympathetic party should straightway be formed for the achievement of the famous mountain, I inwardly hailed it with keen delight, though I felt impelled to respond at first with these words only: —

"Very good. I approve; but I also protest."

Protest? Why protest? and against what? And, if "protest," wherefore "very good"? Would I be kind enough to explain?

Of course I would explain: nothing was easier

than to explain. No inconsiderable part of my career as an excursionist in various parts of the globe had been passed in protesting against precisely the same form of tourist absurdity which long and unvarying experience taught me to foresee impending in the present instance. I had protested alike in Wales, Franconia, Scotland, the Rocky Mountains, Egypt, and Switzerland; always earnestly, often logically, sometimes eloquently, and never successfully. Either the superior resolution of companions, or my own feebleness of will, had invariably overcome me. But, confident of the justice of my convictions, I proceeded to protest once again, — as I shall forever continue to protest, under kindred circumstances, even with the certainty of defeat before me, — with more energy and at greater length than need here be repeated, but to the following effect: —

In preparing for expeditions of the kind now projected, all travellers, whatever their age, station, or place of birth, accept, without consideration or discussion, as a foregone and inevitable conclusion, the fictitious necessity of interrupting the regular habits of their lives, impairing their digestions, embittering their tempers, destroying their powers of observation, and dulling their senses of delight for several hours of the day, by causing themselves to be partially aroused (thorough wakening is impossible) at incongruous and exasperating hours before dawn, and performing superhuman feats of exertion, in the delusion that the grandeurs of nature can be best appreciated and most satisfactorily enjoyed under these abnormal conditions. It almost seems superfluous to expose the fallacy; yet there never was a vagrant pleasure-party, and I suppose there never will be, capable of taking arms against, and, by opposing, ending it. They all seek new sights of beauty or wonder at a time when partial darkness covers the face of the earth, and it is next to impossible to discern a single object. They invite sensations of novelty and freshness in a dazy stupor which stifles all exhilaration and excitement. They deprive themselves of the hours of rest to which they have been accustomed, and, with singular innocence or effrontery, expect to maintain an unfailing flow of high spirits and good temper. They disorganize their systems by anachronistic food, and wonder what has suddenly become of their health and vigor. They defy a whole series of physical by-laws, and, after many wasted days, return from their laborious jaunt dejected,

To Fuziyama and Back. 73

jaded, and retaining only vague and disconnected outlines of recollection, instead of full, unclouded, wholesome memories. And all because of a loose and uninvestigated theory, that, for the tourist, inordinate early rising is "the only correct thing;" all because certain hardy travellers here and there — mostly Englishmen with prodigious muscular endowments, and constitutions capable of gigantic resistance to fatigue — have sometimes accomplished excessive and unnecessary exploits of endurance by abridging their sleep for weeks and months together, and been accepted as examples of a fanciful rule that the pleasures of exploration can be properly pursued in no other way. Because there are Alpine clubs and the like, it seems there shall be no more true and rational summer diversions, but only hurry, discomfort, fruitless toil, exhaustion, and regret.

All this and more I represented to my friends, as we sat around the *débris* of an excellent dinner in one of the Yokohama hotels, with divers ingenious amplifications and apt illustrations, with subtle irony, apophasis, and other powerful expedients of rhetoric; and, as they were pleasantly occupied with comparisons between the flavors of Japanese melons and those of more familiar climes,

I was suffered to proceed uninterrupted to the end, and fancied that this time, at least, I had produced an impression, and had not protested in vain. But, before the echoes of my peroration had died away, a voice arose, calmly proposing, as if no previous word upon the subject had been spoken, that our breakfast should be ordered at four o'clock of the latter part of the coming night, and that we should hold ourselves ready to start promptly at five. The old, old story was told again, — of five o'clock in the morning. The futility of remonstrance was obvious; and I bowed to the ridiculous but inexorable decree of fate, as I had bowed a hundred times before, and am likely to bow a hundred times again. Something was said about the possible difficulty of securing a suitable interpreter, and of obtaining official permission to go beyond the "treaty limits" in so short a time; but these tasks were cheerily undertaken by one of the company, — an old resident, familiar with the necessary processes; and the question was dismissed without debate. Immediate orders were issued for unlimited supplies of every description of canned provisions; and battalions of sturdy posters were engaged by deputy, to precede us with bedding and other impediments which we were led to believe were essential, but the uselessness of which was speedily demonstrated. Thus Fuziyama, a stray suggestion at half-past seven, P.M., was a settled determination at eight, and would begin to be a realization nine hours later. If a doubt crossed our minds, we dispelled it by reflections that we were already close upon the region of Arabian Nights' romance, where superabundant food could be produced in the twinkling of an Aladdin's lamp, and all obstacles to rapid travel overcome in the shake of a Prince Houssain's carpet; and that in these very islands, more than one hundred and fifty years ago, Captain Lemuel Gulliver had done things not less wonderful, on the whole, than those which we were about to accomplish.

It may not have been precisely four o'clock on the morning of the 3d of September when we re-assembled for breakfast; but it was sufficiently early to disqualify the party from any boisterous demonstrations of liveliness, and to relieve the repast from extravagant hilarity of movement. Torpor was the prevailing and almost unconquerable tendency. The candles were few, and the large room was dim and gloomy. The atmosphere was by no means so favorable to confidence in the magic possibilities of Scherazade and Dean Swift as we had found it last night, apart from the circumstance that our faith in Oriental miracles now received a more direct shock. The Governor of Kanagawa could not be found the night before, and the passports were not ready. The interpreter upon whom we had counted was too busily occupied with other affairs to accompany us, as he declared in a polite apologetic note. These unexpected mishaps would naturally compel a slight delay; but then, as the porters with the supplies had not started at their appointed hour, our own detention might not be wholly malapropos. It is a singular thing, but it is strictly true, that as the time required to adjust these little matters passed by, and daylight began to appear, I felt myself wonderfully improving in equanimity; and when, after we thought all was arranged and we might at last set out in earnest, it was discovered that one of our carriage-wheels was broken, and that we must return to the stables for another vehicle, I grew quite buoyant, and would have become amiable on very small provocation. It is not without complacency that I recall my own magnanimity at that particular period. I did not say "I told you so!" in words; nor did I suffer that irritating observation to be legible in my countenance. I never intimated, even remotely, that, if my remonstrance had been heeded, we might have gained at least two extra hours of snug repose. But I thought a great deal upon the subject; and the peace of mind that my reflections afforded me was inexpressible.

These preliminary mishaps having been duly remedied, we found ourselves, at half-past seven o'clock, outside the gates of Yokohama, and rattling briskly along the broad To Kai Do. Whether it was that the practical vindication of my arguments had soothed me, or that drowsiness had been dispelled by the succession of slight disagreements, or that I now felt a hearty satisfaction in knowing that nothing would be lost to sight in the darkness which precedes dawn, all trace of disquietude — of which I need hardly say there was no very serious amount at any time — rapidly vanished, and I felt as free to enjoy the morning ride as the circumstances should warrant.

Our route had been laid out under the guidance of experienced advisers, and was calculated to afford as extensive and as varied a series of adventures as a hasty tour of six or eight days would permit. For some forty miles we were to travel westward by wagon along that same

To Kai Do, long known as one of the extraordinary chain of magnificent avenues, which, constructed centuries ago for communication throughout the empire, at a time when wheeled vehicles were undreamed of, are at this day, in many respects, as suitable and convenient for any kind of passage as most country roads in Europe and America. Their breadth, their evenness, and their solidity are truly astonishing, considering the remote period when they were built, and the years that have passed without their having received any material improvement or repair. And their beauty is as remarkable as their endurance; for they are all flanked with majestic pines, frequently in double rows, which overarch the way for unbroken miles, and, without interrupting the view on each side, afford constant and refreshing shade. This To Kai Do, which I now fairly saw for the first time, and which extends from Sinagawa, a suburb of Tokio, to the outskirts of Kioto, three hundred miles away, is, from its situation, the most important of all; and we were, of course, duly eloquent over the circumstance that we were now in nimble and unimpeded progress upon a thoroughfare not only of national and historical consequence to the Japanese themselves, but also famous as the favorite object of terror to English writers of the previous ten years, who, almost without exception (and entirely without justification), gratified a morbid fancy by picturing it as a veritable Valley of the Shadow of Death.

II.

SEPTEMBER weather, in the part of Japan which we traversed, is the finest of the year. The heaviest summer rains are then over; and the air is deliciously cool, excepting at very mid-day, besides being perfumed with all the freshness of the invigorated fields. Everywhere about us were the signs of careful cultivation in the valleys, and beauties of a wilder nature upon the highlands. Pleasant villages abounded along the road, the inhabitants of which turned for a moment from their tasks, as we passed by, to bestow a hasty salutation. As the morning advanced, the prospect was varied by the gradual rise of the O Yama (great mountain) range, a little to the north. This is a line of hills, the highest of which is some six thousand feet above the sea-level, and which has always borne a particular reputation for sanctity, to that degree, that, until very recent days, foreigners could not approach it except by stealth. We were told that it was thickly covered with temples, and — which was afterward found to be quite true — that staircases reached to its topmost point. But, bent as we were upon scaling a far loftier height, the respectable altitude of O Yama did not much impress us. Our carriage-route took us through several flourishing towns, and over a number of streams, most of which had to be crossed in boats, recent freshets having swollen them so as to make fording impracticable. Until noon our course was wholly inland; but a little after twelve o'clock we came upon the shore of Odawara Bay, one of the great inlets of the principal island, which the To Kai Do skirts for half a dozen miles. At this particular time the bay was in a state of fine agitation; and heavy rollers ten feet high dashed up the beach to the thresholds of the fishermen's cottages that lined the way. While the afternoon was yet early, we reached the bank of the Sakawa River, beyond which, according to the provisions of the treaties, strangers might not pass without especial permission. The rule, however, was merely nominal, and only theoretically adhered to in order that it might be enforced in case of necessity, which has now and then occurred. So far as we were concerned, although properly supplied with passports, we were not even questioned by the guard; nor, indeed, had we occasion to assert our privileges at any time throughout the journey.

During the greater part of the year the Sakawa is a low and narrow stream, or, rather, a collection of streams, winding irregularly through the crevices of a broad bed, which is never really filled except in the seasons of freshets. But, like all the other rivers of this mountainous island, it then rises to extraordinary height and width, and at times becomes impassable. We were fortunate in catching it just at the critical limit. A few inches more, and we might have been obliged to wait, perhaps for days, until the overflow should subside. As it was, the method of crossing was sufficiently hazardous to disturb the nerves of the timid. Being our first opportunity of genuine adventure in Japan, we were bound to welcome it; but some of the natives who undertook the passage at the same time, particularly those of the gentler sex, openly showed themselves as little at their ease, as, possibly, we felt. For each passenger there was a platform of planks about six feet square, the corners of which were taken upon the shoulders of strong porters, who, assisted by long poles, cautiously felt their way through the rapid flood. For a considerable part of the distance the water rose to their armpits, and all their strength was needed to resist the impetuous current. More than once they were obliged to pause and rest, supporting themselves by their staffs, at which times the frail vehicle was lifted, over and again, by the aggressive waves. If they had missed the course of the ford, the consequences might have been serious enough, in such a torrent. But they were never guilty of a misstep; and the worst that happened to anybody was a bath of spray, or the submersion of half an inch of the body, when an unforeseen eddy would flow over the edges of the boards. The crossing occupied nearly half an hour. We all declared that we enjoyed it heartily, and would not have missed it for any consideration; but I did not observe that any regrets were shed over the fact that our return route to Yokohama had been so arranged as to lead us another way.

From the river's side to the town of Odawara, a distance of about a mile, we proceeded on foot, escorted by as many of the youthful population as had become aware of our approach. The demeanor of these juvenile followers was peculiar. So long as they found themselves unnoticed, they surrounded us at every point, scrutinizing us with a minuteness that left no detail of our appearance free from criticism; but, the instant the slightest attention was directed toward them, they fled in confusion and excitement, and rallied only when it appeared that we were once more absorbed in our own concerns. This was at first regarded as mere affectation, and so, undoubtedly, with the youngest it may have been; that is to say, with those whose experience of foreigners had been limited to a single season. The others, I regret to say, had more substantial grounds for their timidity. They had learned that the temper of the Western nations is capricious and untrustworthy; and that behind a smiling exterior a malicious ingenuity often hides. Odawara is not sufficiently remote from the foreign centre to be ignorant of what the roughs of the colony are capable of. The children were shy of us then, and they grow shyer every year. The adults do not much admire us; but they see their way to probable profit as a result of casual intercourse, and do not shrink from the chances of a little ill-treatment. Moreover, they are not absolutely certain of never-ending abuse. They belong to a race of optimists, and perpetually look forward to encountering parties of excursionists who will treat them like human beings. On rare occasions their hopes are gratified; and then they call their friends together, and tell them about it, and the event becomes a topic of conversation for weeks together, throughout the neighborhood.

Our projects did not call for a long delay in Odawara; but there were *kagos*[1] to be hired for those who had faith in their questionable comfort, and native slippers and sandals to be purchased for those who contemplated occasional pedestrian experiments: so an hour of leisure was decreed, and various rambles through the town were undertaken. It was not then a place of the first importance, and fishing was almost the only industry of the population; but it was still the chief town of a large province, and at the time of our visit was the residence of a tolerably powerful *daimio*, — not one of the greatest, but a lord whose annual revenue in prosperous seasons may have been equal in value to a million and a half of dollars. We found his ancient castle with little difficulty, as it stood conspicuous in the centre of the town, and amused ourselves by picturing, in imagination,

[1] *Kagos* were, at the time of which I write, the only popular vehicles in Japan, and to a considerable extent they still remain in use. They are of two kinds, which differ only in trifling details of construction. Those used by the fastidious are square boxes, with regular sliding-doors, windows, and roof: they are commonly called *nori-mono*. The less pretentious consist of a shallow round basket, hung by joints of bamboo from a stout pole. When the article is in use, each end of the pole rests upon the shoulder of a porter. At first view it seems an instrument of hideous torture, and so it often proves to the unaccustomed foreigner; although a Japanese fits himself as contentedly within it as a chicken may be conjectured to fit itself to the interior of a shell.

its now decaying walls and towers in the full glory of mediæval pomp, and crowded with the valorous men-at-arms who perished ages ago in its defence. The interior was not accessible, the last representative of the feudal house of Okubo still maintaining some vestiges of his former state therein. We consoled ourselves, in Æsopian fashion, with the conviction that things inside must be even worse than the exterior; and we were right, although we did not know it then. There is a deal of majesty and stateliness about the walls of the old castles of Japan; but the mansions within, with their myriads of apartments for vassals of every rank, have mostly fallen into ruins, and those which still retain the antique framework and outline are melancholy in their gradual decay. They were to a great extent already deserted at the time of our tour; and, once unoccupied and uncared for by their former owners, they soon ceased to be habitable.

In four of the most spacious *kagos* that the town afforded, we set forth again, and ere long forsook the broad To Kai Do, for a branch road leading more directly to the mountainous region northward. There are various ways of reaching the foot of Fuziyama; and it would be a waste of opportunities to go and return by the same route. We had decided to leave the To Kai Do passage till the last. The pathway which we now ascended was at first spacious, but presently grew so narrow and precipitous as to be practicable only for horses, or such conveyances as we were employing. Here the scenery grew wilder and more strange. The rocky shelf over which we were carried overlooked the river that flows from the Hakone Lake, and rushes into the bay with a force that stirs it to boiling foam. Innumerable tributary streams dashed over the hillsides; and the stony walls that encircled us were curiously cleft at intervals, revealing exquisite glimpses of tranquil valleys beyond. Although we were in bright sunshine, it was evident that heavy rains had preceded us; for we were continually met by reports of pathways obstructed by inundations, and bridges swept away. As long as these tales of mishap did not bear directly upon us, we found in them much matter for diversion, and congratulated ourselves on the unusual features of our progress. But, coming suddenly upon a portentous chasm which imperatively barred our way, and which there could be no hope of crossing, our spirits were modified. It then became necessary to turn back, and seek another gap, over which hung a suspension-bridge consisting of a single rope. From the rope a straw basket was swung, in which we were separately hauled across, with a speed that showed long experience on the part of the natives, and a complete disregard for our want of familiarity with the process. It was doubtless safe enough for those who had been brought up to it, and so, I presume, are the tight-rope exploits of the Blondin tribe; but I think it is more entertaining to remember than it was to go through with. To this day, I cannot recall the tossing and plunging air voyage from cliff to cliff, with the white water raging among the rocks below, and all view of human surroundings shut off by the sinking of the cord, without a feeling of giddiness. It was a relief to learn, on arriving at the other side, that the way to our resting-place for the night was clear from that point. Our passion for adventure and romance was satisfied.

I have no words to convey a sense of the beauty of the landscape, as we proceeded farther among the hills. The old measures of comparison fail entirely in Japan. Superlatives of expression are not needed, nor would they be justified; for there is a more genuine grandeur in Switzerland, and, perhaps, a more nearly perfect grace in many parts of Southern France. But the charm here lies in the constant variety and the unexpected

combinations of opposite extremes. The views
change abruptly, and with kaleidoscopic swiftness. There are towering crags, gloomy abysses,
shining valleys, bleak heaths, and fertile meadows,
all following each other in such close succession as to seem almost a defiance of the common law of nature. As I lay back in my *kago*,
indifferent, that day, to physical constraint, I
found it bewildering and amazing, but inexpressibly lovely. The path was carpeted with thick
mosses, and hedged with bright ferns. At times
it was shaded with arching pines, and at others it
wound along the edges of precipices, beneath
which were clustered pretty villages with rich
farms and dainty gardens. Wild flowers hung
from the rocks, and twined about the shrubbery in
profusion. There were few houses upon the route;
but here and there a red temple peeped from a
thicket of bamboo. Toward evening the ascent
became more rapid; loftier peaks began to rise
around us, and fogs obscured the valleys below:
but even at this altitude we could discern,
through curtains of mist, neat little patches of
rice and tobacco, wherever a level spot had been
found sufficiently broad to be thus utilized. In
consequence of the detention caused by the broken
bridge, it grew quite dark before we could reach

our evening's destination. The sure-footed *kago*-bearers had no need to slaken their pace, and hurried us through the twilight as if the sense of sight were not at all necessary to their security. There was no moon; and, after a little time, nothing was clearly distinguishable on either side. Imagination, however, lined the way with a series of mysterious caverns and grottos, more marvellous, no doubt, than any of those which we had actually seen, and upon which these dim fancies were based. Serenades saluted us from every direction, — the songs of insects[1] (they are not content with humming, but have learned to sing, in this land), the rustling of foliage shaken by the wind, and the echoing fall of countless cascades. Finally, lights were seen, flickering and dancing in our path. Every thing was weird, fantastic,

---

[1] The melodious capabilities of some of the Japanese insects are remarkable. The *semi*, a sort of large locust, carries about with him an apparatus upon which he plays with such shrill emphasis as to delude the inexperienced stranger into a belief that he is listening to a bird of great size and power. Sometimes he executes a long and plaintive wail, with a pathetic "dying fall," and sometimes emits a cheery note, like a jovial whistle. It is not really a vocal operation at all, but a curious instrumental performance. The *suzu mushi* (or bell-insect) is even more peculiar. In the summer evenings he fills the air with sounds like that of a sharp, clear stroke upon a tiny bell, or like a prolonged jingling of the same. The illusion is perfect; not merely a resemblance, but seems a positive identity.

unreal, in that strange scene. It is elfin-land, even in the estimation of the Japanese themselves; and these forests are filled with ghostly legends. Were these, then, goblin lamps, to lure us to confusion, perhaps to dire catastrophe? Nothing of the sort. They were friendly lanterns, sent out by our advance-guard of porters, to cheer the last opaque half-mile, and to notify us of our near approach to the famous baths of Miyanoshita. *Kago*-carriers and torchmen united in choruses of enthusiastic glee; the march was again quickened, and, ten minutes later, we entered the village inn, four generations of the proprietor's family meeting us at the door, and welcoming us with low bows and jubilant acclamations.

III.

MIYANOSHITA enjoys a high repute, not only for the advantages of its situation, but also for hot mineral springs, which are said to possess rare healing qualities. The latter we had no occasion to test, and of the former it was impossible to judge at the late hour of our arrival. We found it convenient only, to exhaust the contents of certain cans, and dispose ourselves in comfortable positions for repose. Each traveller had a window to himself, looking out upon a tempting vista of woods and waters, half lighted by the moon, which had now risen. But the fatigues of the day were irresistible, and the bewitching reality soon gave place to dreamy visions. There was no appreciable difference between the waking and sleeping impressions. I suppose it is only in Japan that one can rouse himself from the fantasies of the night, and confront the facts of morning, without serious disappointment. Dreams are not often so enchanting as the outlook from the Miyanoshita windows at sunrise.

Fair as it was, we could give but little time to

it; for every hour, at this period of the year, might add to the difficulties of ascending Fuziyama. It was essential that we should reach the foot of the mountain that night. So, after hastily breakfasting, and taking leave of our host, his grandmother, mother, wife, and troop of children, we coiled into the *kagos*, to which we were becoming inured, and started upon the passage of the Hakone range, which interposes, like a Titanic wall, between the eastern provinces and the solitary giant of Suruga. For a while, this barrier hid the loftier peak; but, as we steadily mounted, the sharp and regular cone appeared again, as perfect in the exactness of its proportions as when seen from the greatest distances. From the highest point of these inferior hills, perhaps four thousand feet above the sea-level, we had the first unbroken view of the entire mass of Fuziyama. But for a single protrusion on the southern slope, caused by an eruption a century and a half ago, the smooth curve is unvarying from the summit to the base. In spite of enormous bulk and towering height, this evenness of outline gives an appearance of delicacy and softness which can never be dissociated from it. Gentleness and serenity seem always to be its crowning attributes. The rugged vigor of the mountains of Europe and North America declares them of a wholly different type.

The second day was less eventful than the first, and the progress was slower. We found abundant reason to admire the strength and endurance, and, above all, the good spirits, of our *kago*-men, who made light of a labor which seemed to us superhuman. They laughed and sang as merrily when lifting us at incredible angles over acclivities which could only be surmounted by literally climbing from step to step, as if they had been strolling on level ground for their mere pleasure: we found it impossible, for our part, to accomplish a mile on foot without any burden at all. When we arrived at comparatively level ground, we relieved them by walking; but this did not seem to increase their comfort to any extent, and they were always quite as ready to receive us back as we were to be taken in. More than once they would start of their own choice, and trot with us up a steep incline the simple sight of which was almost enough to take our breath away.

Late in the afternoon we came to the town of Subasiri, from which the ascent on the eastern side of the mountain usually begins. This, however, is only a matter of ancient custom, which tourists will in due time reform, since better points of departure can be found much farther on. But Subasiri is a place of note, and has a temple of considerable renown, from which pilgrims receive spiritual encouragement before taking the final steps toward the accomplishment of their mission. It has a comfortable inn and a hospitable population, the young men of which gambolled on the green, after dinner, for our diversion. Among other sports they attempted a wrestling match. We had heard much of Japanese wrestling, and watched the exhibition with curiosity. But there was little skill displayed; and in fact one of our own party, mingling in the good-humored fray, overthrew the champion with scarcely an effort. Whereupon they declared that they were only amateurs, and that their sole purpose was to afford entertainment to the visitors.

The following day was to be devoted to the supreme effort, and it is needless to say that the mania of midnight starting again possessed my ambitious companions. If arguments were unavailing in Yokohama, it would have been still more useless to proffer them here. An early bed did not bring quick repose, certain obstacles to slumber having, up to this time, evaded such exterminating processes as the innholder of Subasiri has brought to bear upon them. Nevertheless, at half-past two in the morning we were called together; and at three we stumbled drowsily forth, fortunate, at least, in a fine moon, which enabled us to distinguish the road which we were to pursue. Fuziyama was dimly perceptible; but nobody praised it, and nobody found it attractive. How could any mountain make itself engaging to senses depressed and benumbed as ours were? As a simple matter of course, we all dropped into our *kagos* after having walked half a dozen rods, and next dropped into sound sleep, from which nothing could disturb us until we were deposited at the spot where the ascent on foot always begins.

I here remark, for the benefit of future explorers who may desire to climb this celebrated mountain, but shrink from its hardships, that the labor is needlessly increased by following the custom of the natives, and abandoning the *kago* at the first approach to elevated ground. It always has been done; and as the Japanese, especially in the rural districts, are remarkable for their fidelity to precedents, they assume that it always must be done. I believe there is no sort of unwillingness to afford every accommodation that might be asked for; but strangers, of course, do not know what they are likely to require, and trust blindly to the assurances of their guides. A person who had once accomplished the feat would understand exactly how to proceed; but nobody attacks Fuziyama a second time. The new-comer, being told positively that it is necessary to walk from a given point, because everybody does the same, gives no thought to the matter, and does as he is advised. The truth is, that, for many miles up the mountain-side, the way is freer from difficulties than the path over the hills of Hakone, which are always crossed in *kagos*. What is more, if horses were employed, the toil of more than one-half of the ascent could be wholly avoided. I have sometimes contemplated, more or less seriously, a repetition of this trip on purpose to show how easily it might be done; but on reflection have concluded that it was better to offer the practical counsel than to make the personal sacrifice. So here I announce to all excepting those who take a pride in extravagant achievements of pedestrianism, that with the help of a little persuasion and some resolution, just sufficient to overcome an old prejudice, and secure the co-operation of any stable proprietor in the locality, two-thirds of the pathway to the summit of Fuziyama may be traversed with no greater difficulty than Mount Washington in New Hampshire, or even little Snowdon in Wales.

In our complete ignorance, we surrendered the vehicles at the first suggestion, and made the usual purchases of stout poles, which are sold in a little wayside temple on the pretence that they greatly facilitate the work of ascending. This is another illusion of mountain-travelling, which flourishes in every part of the world where mountains exist. I do not know what it may be to those who are familiar with such labors; but, to the uninitiated, the staff is more of a hindrance than a help. In the first place, the energies of the holder are exhausted in the endeavor to invent methods of making it effective; in the next, its mere weight, however slender it may be, becomes a serious burden at that inevitable time when the sharp angles of ascent make the pilgrim impatient of each superfluous ounce. But everybody takes a pole; and so, of course, did we. I presume, after all, that it did not retard our progress more than a quarter of a mile an hour. The sun was rising while we arranged this little matter of outfit, and we could not resist the temptation to delay and watch its action upon the peak above us. First, the pile of cold gray deepened to a thick and heavy tint, like lead; the prominent lines of the sides and top alone being touched by a dull, ruddy hue, with little sign of life or brightness.

Presently purple shadows began to pass from point to point, faint and flickering for a while, afterward firmer and deeper, until the whole broad cone was richly suffused with a tranquil and tender color that seemed to wait only for a kindling spark to flash into luminous vitality. But the changes were yet measured and gradual. Delicate lines of violet crept irregularly down the slopes, as uncertain in their course, and indefinable, as the waves of the Polar Lights. Then bolder rays succeeded; the vast bulk contracted with the growing distinctness; and, suddenly enough at last, as the sun rose from the horizon behind us, the summit burst into a blaze like living flame. This flood of dazzling light threw all beneath into deep shadow again; and for many minutes the line of demarcation was sharp and abrupt, like a black shore receding before a tide of fire. There was no interval of gradation between the fierce glow above and the heavy gloom below. With the further rising of the sun, this phenomenon disappeared, and, before long, all that was visible of mountain-top became a radiant mass, darting strange gleams of changing brilliancy, as startling in their quick mutations as those of a huge opal. It was incredible that a great barren pyramid of rock and cinder could be so swiftly turned to such a miracle of half-transparent lightness and iridian beauty. Few effects like it are possible in this world: perhaps the same effect is nowhere else possible; for it needs the unusual combination of a mountain of extraordinary height and yet free from snow, the entire absence of rival intervening peaks which would break the overwhelming rush of sunlight, and an atmosphere purer than Europe or the inhabited parts of America ever know.

With the exception of one little depression near the starting-point, where a descent of a few feet is necessary to cross a ravine, the rise, from beginning to end, is uninterrupted. For some miles it is gradual; and we did not find it too fatiguing, so long as we carried our poles over the shoulder, and made no attempts to use them. The way was almost entirely our own. A fortnight earlier, we should have had the companionship of thousands of pilgrims; for Fuziyama, during the months of July and August, is crowded with devotees from all parts of the country, who flock to its summit with no special religious purpose, but with the general conviction that it is an act of piety which will bring its own reward in some undefined way. The visits for this year were at an end; although one little party of four passed us in the morning,

To Fuziyama and Back. 101

and found their way to the top with a speed that we approved, but could not emulate. There is a general impression that women are not permitted to ascend Fuziyama; but there were certainly two young girls in this native quartet of which I speak. None of them wore the regular pilgrim's dress of white cotton; but all, the girls included, were clad in a sort of page-like attire, which, with the trousers rolled far above the knees, was suggestive of some of the epicene costumes of the burlesque stage. As these active damsels skipped by, we gazed upon their robust legs, not so much with admiration as with envy. It was clear that there would be no premature giving out on their part; and I may as well here admit, that, long before we had finished our upward work of that day, we saw them descending by another route, having performed the whole operation while we were yet in the preliminary stages. But the elastic endurance of these Japanese is something of which we have hardly a conception; and for a foreigner to lament his inability to equal their exploits would be an endless waste of time.

Vegetation rapidly disappears upon the sides of Fuzi; and, at the height of four thousand feet, little is seen around the path but rough pebbles, lumps of lava, and fields of ashes. But there are no difficulties worth thinking of, until, at about eight thousand feet, the first of the line of ten halting-places, provided for the comfort of weary travellers, is reached. These convenient stations are situated at tolerably regular distances from one another; and two or more stone cottages have been built at each. They serve the purposes of little hostelries during the season; but all were closed, and the doorways walled up, at our time. They begin at the point where it is supposed that roadside reliefs are necessary to soften the increasing labors of the journey; although, in fact, many of them may be passed before the heavy strain sets in. It was obvious to us, that horses might be used for a considerable distance beyond. We were not experts in this sort of work; but we felt nothing like exhaustion until after passing the fifth station, and then we knew that we had nearly reached our limit. There were soaring spirits among us, who talked, with resolution, of striding to the summit before nightfall; but, though their voices were firm, their knees shook visibly in contradiction. Strong differences of opinion arose; but these were evenly adjusted, in good season, by natural processes. The weaker ceased to discuss, and pulled themselves along with silent determination to prolong the struggle to a certain altitude, and then to put in the most effective form of passive resistance by lying down and going to sleep. The stronger assumed an exuberance which they did not truly feel, by way of offering an encouraging example, and so wrought upon themselves by loud argument and feats of activity, that, contrary to their will and expectation, they suddenly shut up, not "in measureless content," but like jack-knives, and confessed themselves conquered. It was at "Number Eight" that this conclusion was arrived at. There were still several hours of daylight, but none of us, excepting our guides, to the manner born, were fit to utilize them; and a vote for postponement of further operations until dawn of the next day was carried without dissent.

IV.

"NUMBER EIGHT" is a station of some consequence among its fellows. It has quite a cluster of stone huts, and undoubtedly contains a floating population of several hundred sleepers during the liveliest weeks of summer. Of course, we found it totally deserted. Without much difficulty, — we were ready enough to labor with our arms, — the stones which blocked the door of the principal *châlet* were pulled aside, and abundant space for shelter was dimly revealed, together with a large supply of firewood, which there was reason to believe we might need before the morning. What we did not discover, although we looked for it rather earnestly, was water. Our pioneers had thought it was possible that some of the tanks might have been left partially full; but not a drop could be found. This was a serious disappointment; inasmuch as we had been so confidently assured we could reach the top, and descend again, in a single day, that we had brought a very limited supply of refreshments of any kind. The absence of solid food was not so important a matter; and, indeed, we still had an odd crumb or two left: but we no sooner knew that we were destitute of water than everybody forthwith experienced a raging thirst. While we were debating, with some uneasiness, the possible consequences of this miscalculation, one of the escort astonished us by proposing to go up to the summit, where there was a perennial well, and fetch us as many bottlesful as we wanted. He was pretty sure he could find the well: he had drank at it a hundred times, and, though it might be dark, he could probably feel his way to it. We suggested, that, in case he failed, it would be a pity to have taken so much trouble for nothing; to which he answered, that it was a trifle, and that he would be back, with or without water, before bedtime. Whereupon, stimulated by this display of enterprise, another attendant remarked that our box of edibles was nearly empty, and that he thought he could not do better than go back to Subasiri, and replenish it. This time we did remonstrate in earnest; but he laughed at the idea of there being any thing heroic in the undertaking, and declared he should find it a very pleasant midnight jaunt. When he saw to what degree he had surprised us, he grew very proud of his proposition, and drew so merry a picture, we were informed, of the sensation he should produce at the tavern by breaking in at two in the morning, that we saw no occasion for making any further objections on his account — on our own, it is needless to say, we were delighted. As the water-seeker started away in one direction, he set forth in the other, pledging himself to be back, sufficiently laden, in time for our breakfast.

We had now nothing to do but enjoy ourselves with such prospects as the great elevation afforded us; and, although we were on the wrong side of the mountain for the most striking effects of sunset, we found enough to give us hour after hour of uninterrupted wonder and delight. The surface of the country was totally hidden by clouds, and it was with the singular transformations and illusions of these veils of vapor that our attention was occupied. It was the more fortunate for us, since nothing in the real panorama could have equalled the fanciful images that spread themselves before us. The land-view from a very lofty mountain is seldom of itself remarkably fascinating. There is a sense of majesty in the prodigious expanse, but there are no details for the eye to rest upon. After a certain height, the individual forests, lakes, and smaller hills, all disappear, or melt into what seems like a broad circle of rolling waves. From greater heights, the waves appear more subdued; and from the greatest the scene has all the dead tranquillity of the ocean in a calm. Excepting in places where the air is as clear as in Japan, there is much more to be gained by ascending low mountains than high ones. The picture from Montanvert is lovely; but I wonder if anybody ever felt a genuine gratification in being at the top of Mont Blanc, except that of having triumphed over a host of difficulties and dangers, and accomplished a feat which is still considered worthy of immortality in "The London Times." All mountain-views, after a certain point, are much alike, and it is only when they are seen through an extremely favorable medium that they present any special or distinctive characteristics. Take away its own peculiar atmosphere from Fuziyama, and it would be no better worth surmounting than the highest peaks of Europe. As it is, it has qualities which will always recommend it, even to tourists who have gauged the resources of half the famous mountains of the globe.

Against the background of the horizon, we beheld that evening such spectacles of cloud-pageantry as none of us would have believed the earth could show. All that was marvellous in form and color, more than the imagination could have summoned, was set before us with a splendor, that, to our unaccustomed eyes, seemed supernatural. It was not with a feeling of calm satisfaction that we gazed upon these visions, but of vivid excitement. They lasted long after the hour of sunset in lower regions, and until we were driven within walls by the increasing cold. The wind was sharp and bitter after the sunlight had wholly disappeared; and we were glad to avail ourselves of the protection which the rough architects of "Number Eight" had supplied.

It was soon necessary to make use of the stores of fuel left by the late occupants. Even in midsummer the rigors of the nights require artificial heat; and now, in September, we should have suffered severely without it. Our prudent attendants had matches and candles; and in a short time we were gathered about a brisk wood-fire, kindled on the bare ground, in the centre of the hut. The construction of these mountain-retreats is primitive. They consist of four stone walls and a flat roof of boards, on top of which are piled bowlders and blocks of lava, to keep the lighter substance from flying away in high winds. They have no chimneys or windows; and the door is of the narrowest possible dimensions. The first consequence, therefore, of a fire, is a thick and pervading smoke, which packs itself into every crevice of the interior before finding its way through the scanty apertures of the eaves and corners. This dreadful smoke increased our thirst, which was a new distress; but, on the other hand, it broke up our appetite, which was a benefit, in view of our short stock of provisions. At nine o'clock we heard hilarious cries without; and presently, through the double darkness, the form of Aquarius disclosed itself. He was welcomed with a fervent drinking-chorus. He had scaled the heights, found the well, broken its covering of ice, filled his bottles, and returned, all in about three hours. We were able, the next day, to estimate the merits of this exploit.

We divided such food as remained to us with our native companions, and united in an effort to make a comfortable arrangement of our quarters for the night. The only coverings we could get together were one travelling-rug, a *kago*-cushion, and two Mackintosh overcoats. Watches were set to keep the fire in undiminished force; but they were not fairly maintained: and we underwent the pleasing changes of alternate fierce glow and decaying flicker until morning. The dreamy transitions from Greenland's icy mountains to

India's coral strands impaired the temper, and to some extent enfeebled the sense of integrity, of the party. Whenever the cold became intolerable to any one in particular, he would rise, fling an armful of loose wood upon the embers, steal an overcoat from the soundest sleeper, and turn over again to uneasy repose. The Japanese, however, appeared to suffer little disturbance. In one respect, this was difficult to understand. That they should remain insensible to the cold, being by habit inured to exposure, was in the natural order of things; but how they could breathe the tranquil slumbers of the blest, with their feet and legs among the coals (into which position some of them had worked themselves), was a problem which recollections of the Book of Martyrs would not help to solve. Of course, it was a miserable night. No consciousness of adventure can keep the spirits alive in the face of unutterable weariness; and the conceit of lying ten thousand feet above the earth does not compensate for the want of wholesome sleep. And tossing restlessly upon bare lava, inhaling smoke and cinders, and riding Walpurgis steeds for broken periods of half an hour each, is not sleep. Occasionally I ventured forth, and tried to soothe myself with glimpses of the moon; but the air was too eager, and nipped away all my enthusiasm before I could get it into working order.

There was no dispute upon the question of early rising the next day. I, sole member of the usual opposition, was this time as ready as any to meet the dawn half way. If persuasion had been needed, I was bursting with arguments to prove that the whole glorious aim of our expedition would be frustrated, if we failed to see that particular morning "flatter the mountain-tops with sovereign eye." But we were all of one mind. Any thing to get away from the tribulations of "Number Eight." Undoubtedly we were unjust to that well-meaning station. It did the best it could for us; and what we must have endured without its shelter cannot be thought of now with composure. We could not see its solid merits in a fair light at the time: so at three o'clock we shook the ashes from our feet, and resumed our ambitious toil. It was not entirely dark; but dense clouds shut off the view below, and the only direct sign of light was a faint russet tinge upon the eastern horizon. From the first, the ascent was far more difficult than any thing we had gone through with the day before. I think the great fatigue of Fuziyama is not especially owing to its steepness and frequent irregular abruptness, although these are painful enough, but rather to the circumstance that there is never any variation or relief from the steady upward course. Other mountains have their little caprices of level or decline; but here there is none. The strain is never for a moment relaxed; and the angle near the summit is so sharp, that it is next to impossible to stop even for a moment's rest. Excepting at the halting-places "Number Nine" and "Number Ten," the effort of standing still and keeping a foothold in the loose cinder, or upon the slippery rock, is greater than that of pushing constantly forward. We had little opportunity of turning back to watch the changes of the approaching sunrise; but all that we could see was repetition of the superb effects of the previous evening. When, at last, the sun came in full sight, the rainbow splendors of the scene disappeared. We were surrounded on all sides by a daze of glittering white, with no solidity of substance or color anywhere apparent, except the isolated fragment upon which we stood. The very mountain-top seemed floated from its foundation.

We reached the highest point at seven o'clock. Then the clouds had rolled away; and for a short time we had around us the broad circle of sea and land, including no less than thirteen provinces, which Fuziyama commands when the upper air is cleared, and the lower strata are unburdened with vapors. The prodigious sweep and comprehensiveness of the view were deeply impressive; but the distribution of the landscape was quite undistinguishable. In many directions, the face of the country seemed like a prairie, although we knew it to be as uneven as any in the world. The most striking of the distant objects was the jagged outline of the southern coast, which, for leagues in the neighborhood, was deposited and shaped by this very volcano, in its days of life. But nothing remote could well compel attention here. The mountain itself had the absorbing claim; and it was long before the immeasurable solemnity of its desolation and solitude could be disturbed by consideration of the details which contribute to its grandeur. Our senses were under the spell of an awful gloom; which is indeed, at all times and to all persons, the controlling influence of the scene.

Yet there were details which must not be slighted, and which, when we contrived to turn our minds toward them, we found full of interest. The crater, barren of flame for ages, and now filled up to within six hundred feet of the summit; the village of low huts that stretches almost entirely around its edge; and the groups of images of Buddha, in stone and bronze, that were planted in every accessible open space, — all received due attention, although I think that I would have preferred abandoning these minutiæ, and clinging to the first impressions of the gigantic whole. The truly lasting and memorable effect is that of the circuit around the summit, — a walk of three miles, — which shows the long lines of the descent in every aspect. They are much alike on all sides; and their almost identical precision is one of the strange characteristics of the peak. From the summit, as from below, the cone is nearly perfect. We were fortunate in our morning, and had nothing to interrupt our observations while we remained. The plains below were soon shut out of sight; but that was a minor matter, as I have endeavored to explain. Contrary to our expectation, there was no wind; and the temperature was mild, even warm. Nothing broke the silence but the sound of our own voices, and, once, the shrill scream of a hawk that flew over us.

V.

AT nine o'clock we turned our faces downward. The descent was principally by a different route from the winding, zigzag course by which we had mounted, — more direct, and far more rapid. It ran for a considerable distance through a little ravine, the bed of which was filled with powdery cinder, and along which it was possible to slide for rods together, without danger or very great discomfort. To climb up by such a path would have been out of the question ; and it is never used except for the return. The descending progress was simple, though at first embarrassing in its arbitrary manner of relieving the traveller from all responsibility. He had only to advance his foot, — either foot, — and the operation would take care of itself for a series of yards. The foot would disappear, as in a quicksand, a luxurious sensation of bird-like flight would follow ; and the foot, — either foot, — emerging into view, gave notification of the necessity for a new departure. In this way, a single step was sometimes sufficient to propel one a dozen times his own length.

116 Japanese Episodes.

The only peril was that of collision, and this was frequently inevitable. No amount of activity, no vigor of stride, could enable the light weights to hold their own, or check the career of the more ponderous who came in contact with them. The race was not to the swift or the strong, but to the heavy.

We might have continued in this easy way for some miles, but for the need of turning aside, and regaining our "Number Eight," where the messenger for food, who had left us the night before, was to rejoin us. He was on hand, and had already been waiting half an hour. It seemed to us the most amazing thing we had ever heard of, entirely overshadowing the feat of the water-bearer; but the unwearied climber insisted that it was nothing worth alluding to, and said that the hope of sharing in the division of the spoils had amply sustained him throughout. He was rewarded with beer, at the sight of which one of his comrades darted off with a sprightly purpose in his eye, beseeching us to drink nothing until his return. We saw him winding among the cliffs for a few minutes, and then lost sight of him; but soon he re-appeared, and, after sundry antelope bounds, stood again among us, bearing a distended cloth, the which, on being laid open, was found to contain a fine lump of the purest snow. It was worth its weight in thanks, and we did not hesitate to say so. We even said it in Japanese; a certain form of polite acknowledgment being one of the most frequent ejaculations of this courteous race, and, consequently, one of the most quickly grasped by strangers.

While we sat and breakfasted, we were surprised by the appearance of a couple of foreign tourists who had come still a day later than ourselves in the season. These were Baron Richtofen, the eminent scientist, and Dr. Wagener, one of the most earnest and generous laborers in the intellectual development of the youth of Japan that Europe has supplied. I was not at that time aware that either of these gentlemen possessed a single claim to consideration; and as they told us they had left Subasiri only at three that morning, and that they meant to thoroughly explore the summit, and descend before night, they produced in my mind no feeling but that of extreme bitterness. It was exasperating to hear a pair of pedestrians talk so cavalierly of accomplishing in less than eighteen hours what had cost us, or would cost us, nearly two laborious days. But one of the twain afterward became an excellent friend of mine; and before I left Japan, three years later, I formally forgave him.

The truth undoubtedly is, that, to experienced mountaineers, Fuziyama presents no difficulties equal to those which may be found, by those who choose to search for them, among the Alpine ranges ; and its ascent and descent in a single day is not a task of heroic dimensions. What our Japanese guides did, of their own free will, showed the rate at which they valued the labor of running up and down. But, in the record of our expedition, I have had to deal with four individuals of merely ordinary endowments of fibre and endurance, — of a kind that will represent the majority of excursionists in the same direction. Speaking to such, I warn them against being led astray by the representations of hardened experts, or of agile natives. Let them try Fuziyama, by all means ; it is one of the "sensations" of a lifetime ; but let them never dream of giving less than two days to the work, and let them bear well in mind the valuable hints hereinbefore set down with regard to the usefulness of equine aid up to a point far beyond any yet attained with the consent of the inhabitants.

I think that breakfast at "Number Eight" ranks first of all among the memorable repasts of many lands. We were all faint with hunger, to begin with ; and that is better than all the piquant sauces of the Boulevards, Regent Street, or Fifth Avenue. And the meal itself was by no means contemptible. We had rice, eggs, potatoes, potted ham and beef, green corn, tea, and beer, — incongruous, perhaps, but with many a lively charm of unexpectedness. We ate till close upon noon, and then took leave of "Number Eight" in a far more charitable humor than that which inspired us at early morning. It was a dreary hovel then; and now we thought of it only as a cosey wayside retreat, an eligible snuggery, the sort of place to go and pass a week in. Turning off to one side, we resumed our sliding descent, until the approach to solid beds of lava, and the occasional interference of sharp ledges, admonished us to caution. Here our guides good-naturedly proposed to assist us with their broad shoulders, and they offered themselves so simply and smilingly, that everybody was glad to accept. As a general rule, there is something intensely objectionable in suggestions of this sort. A Swiss does it in an offensively patronizing way; a South-American Indian cringes horribly; an Arab, in the Pyramids, holds out his hand, and you can see the palm itching as he extends it, — he exults avariciously over your weakness, as the occasion for pressing small pecuniary demands upon you.

Each time he offers to take hold of you, you feel that it is from a grasping motive in the wrong sense. A Japanese wants to help you because you are tired, and unused to the exertion; and it is the most natural thing in the world for him to lend a little of his superfluous strength. Therefore, it is a satisfaction to cling to him. Especially as he is clean. The Arab of the Pyramids is never clean. It is the prerogative of guides in most countries to be otherwise.

It was still early in the afternoon when we reached the place where we had left our *kagos* the morning before. They were waiting to receive us, and, as a matter of inevitable custom, hailed us with a heartiness, that, in other lands, would not have been inappropriate if we had been their steadfast and liberal patrons for years. The return to Subasiri was rapidly accomplished; and the splashing revelry of hot and cold baths absorbed all attention for a considerable period. Then followed dinner, and afterward the formal auditing and settlement of accounts with the innkeeper. His charges, though not inordinate, were eccentric. We found, for example, the article of fine weather set down as an important item. It did not appear probable, that, even in the interior of a country of such strange possibilities as Japan, fine weather could really be bought and sold like more controllable commodities: so we demanded an explanation. We were informed that Fuziyama, being a mountain of more or less sacred attributes, was subject to the influences of the priests who are settled at its base; and that they, having been duly applied to, had exercised their charms and spells to prolong the clear and favorable weather for our benefit. The sum was to be transferred to them, not retained by the host for his own uses. Discussion upon this topic would have been laborious: so the financial knot was cut by striking out the questionable item without debate. The amendment was accepted without a remonstrance, — even smilingly; from which we inferred that the expedient had probably been tried before, and found equally ineffective. These claims duly adjusted, we were ready enough for an early bed; but I, at least, could not secure sleep at the first or second invitation. The excessive fatigue, and the recollection of the vast variety of new experiences, combined to keep me from more than a drowsy inertia. All the night long I wandered over hills and valleys of fantastic imagination, scaling immeasurable heights, plunging into fathomless abysses, suffering unlimited pangs of hunger and thirst, shrinking appalled before the most trifling obstacles of exploration, and triumphing with a simple impulse of the will over the wildest impossibilities. Toward morning, I became deeply involved in the landscapes represented upon the dimly-lighted screens around me. They were complicated beyond description, and embraced scenes of startling incongruity, such as could never have had existence except in the mind of a most fanciful artist; but I followed them in all their intricate windings, and, before dawn, was familiar with every detail of their topography. I was greatly pleased with them, and had settled upon a place of residence in one of them, which I had thoroughly decided not to quit for a fixed number of years, when the flitting forms of the tavern domestics aroused me to full consciousness, and dragged me from my peaceful retirement in the heart of a Japanese screen.

VI.

MANY roads lead to Fuziyama, and we had naturally determined to vary our journey by selecting a different returning route from that through which we had come. We would abandon the valley of Miyanoshita, and make a circuit by the way of Hakone Lake, — a very famous sheet of water in native legend and poetry. Before starting, however, I became conscious of a duty to be performed. An exposition of generosity came upon me. The guide who had propped and sustained me during the latter part of my downward mountain progress must be rewarded by my own words, my own smile, and a pecuniary token from my own hand. He was summoned, and I addressed him in what I think may be aptly called modified English. He seemed interested, and his countenance brightened, especially at the moment when the pecuniary token touched his palm. "Observe, fellow-countryman," said I to one of our party, "observe the quick intelligence of this man. He understands me perfectly. He knows my motive, and is grateful. I am pleased with him. I will give him another coin."

The fellow-countryman appealed to, who was as new to Japan as myself, agreed cordially that it was a most interesting incident; but another companion, an old resident, and consequently a scoffer, remarked that anybody would understand the offer of a bit of money, and that it did not require an apprehension of the highest order to look alive, and hold out his hand, under such circumstances.

Feeling pained, but still confident, I pushed the question of mutual understanding a little further, and tapped the man on both shoulders, to remind him more acutely of the precise service he had rendered me, and of the obligation I had intended to requite. To my amazement, he instantly dropped upon his knees, and bowed his head to the ground.

The sceptic laughed a hardened and derisive laugh. "He thinks you want him to kneel, and thank you in the regular Japanese way: that is all that enters his mind."

"It may be so," said I with a sigh; "but still I hope the question is susceptible of discussion.

Nevertheless, we did not discuss it.

Our objective point for the day was the town of Misima, once a commercial station, on the To

Kai Do, of considerable importance, though now sadly faded from its former prosperity. The road was more level than those over which we had passed upon our approach to Fuziyama, and presented on all sides the richest evidences of fertility and plenty. From beginning to end, it was a lovely panorama of neat villages, terraced rice-fields, and groves of bamboo and palm, here and there dotted with residences of wealthier holders of the soil, surrounded by ample parks and flower-gardens. Still languishing a little under our recent fatigue, we lounged lazily in the *kagos* throughout the day, in various experimental and unromantic attitudes, sometimes touched with remorse at the uninterrupted labors we were imposing upon our carriers, but speedily consoled by their constant hilarity, and the consciousness that any of their class would be glad enough to exchange places with them for the sake of their profitable job. The view of Misima, in the middle of the afternoon, roused us to active observation. It had not, at that period, ceased to be a busy and thriving town, and it was more conspicuous for cleanliness and beauty than I believe it is at this day. Possessing exceptional water-privileges, its outskirts were crowded with little mills and factories; its houses were of greater size than any we had seen since leaving Yokohama; and in a broad open space at the centre, we discovered a temple of far more imposing dimensions and brilliant adornment than we had before encountered. A remarkable peculiarity was the existence of running streams through many of the thoroughfares, suggesting recollections of Salt Lake City, although here the watercourses were deeper, and more carefully walled in, to prevent their intrusion upon the footways. We passed through an avenue of tall pines into the To Kai Do, which divides the place in half, and thence into the most agreeable hostelry that our journey had yet revealed to us. Its situation, of course, was not to be compared to that of the Miyanoshita inn; but it had unrivalled charms of its own, — an interior which was not only spacious, but which was ingeniously contrived, by some artifice of architecture, to appear far more comprehensive than it really was; decorations, in every hall and passage, of genuine artistic merit; singular cleanliness; and a system of management which indicated high culture and prolonged experience in the practice of hotel-keeping. We were informed that it was a "*daimios*' tavern;" that is to say, when the annual progress of the *daimios* to Yedo was still a custom, this house was one of their regular resting-places. As the journeys of those lordly gentlemen had ceased some years before, there was no longer any necessity for holding in reserve the special apartments once devoted to them; and so we were installed in the *daimios'* room, which we straightway proceeded to occupy, and in which we disposed ourselves in a manner which might have been more familiar than feudal, but which, we were convinced, was much better suited to the relief of the weary senses than the aristocratic formalities to which the spot had in ancient times been consecrated. We lounged industriously, assiduously, with all the might that was left to us, stirring only to take advantage of the changes of view which the various open doors and windows afforded;—one, an exquisite garden, elaborated to the last degree of miniature effect; another, the commercial thoroughfare, its shops covered with strange placards and sign-boards, one of which, weather-beaten and half illegible, was in the Dutch language, and announced supplies of foreign medicines,—a sign that had been carved and painted perhaps three hundred years ago, when the Hollanders travelled freely along the high roads, and left some traces of civilization as partial compensation for the miseries they helped to bring upon the country; a third, — now and always the most attractive anywhere within a hundred miles, — the peak of Fuziyama, unchanged in the symmetry of its form, though seen from a totally new point of observation. I suppose none of us who formed that little body of excursionists will ever forget the Misima "*yado-ya*" and its surroundings. For my own part, I envy those who were destined never to revisit it. It fell to my lot to inhabit it once again, two years later, when I found it only the wreck of its former self. The march of improvement in Japan had left it stranded on the past.

A walk about the suburbs supplied, in 1870, and does at the present time, although the place has lost a part of its old activity, as good an opportunity as could be desired to examine the system of Japanese life and subsistence as it exists in the townships, and, with certain modifications, throughout the empire. The methods of mutual support, the expedients of exchange, the remarkable self-sustaining powers of a single locality, are nowhere better exhibited. Like many other districts in these islands, Misima and its adjacent hamlets form, in a certain sense, a little commonwealth by themselves. They do engage in some manufactures which are sent elsewhere; but their chief occupation seems to be to relieve themselves from any possibility of burdensome dependence upon distant regions. This instinct of self-maintenance may have had its origin in feudal times, when it was the first necessity of each province to make sure of its own faculty of protecting itself in case of aggressive rivalry, or downright hostility, on the part of its neighbors. Whatever the cause, its continuance is of inestimable advantage to the humbler classes of Japan. To it and its outworkings may be traced the absence of want and social degradation which distinguish the race. Every member of a compact community finds an employment of some sort, and each has his claim to respectability in the fact that he is a recognized contributor to the comfort and welfare of the neighborhood. In the fields, factories, workshops, and warehouses of this happy valley, the common object appeared to be to secure the complete production of all that would satisfy the various needs of the inhabitants on the spot, — to provide a supply of every thing, not absolutely forbidden by natural laws, that the wants of the people should demand.

VII.

At noon we moved eastward toward Hakone, upon the reports concerning which we based high expectations. Our road was now the broad To Kai Do, again lined with lofty and arching pines. At a little distance from Misima, its easy level disappeared, and a series of abrupt ascents led the way once more to the heights, which, at a farther distance north, we had traversed three days before. It is not difficult to understand the admiration with which the old Dutch writers dwelt upon this fine thoroughfare. Two hundred years ago, it must have been a marvel to European eyes; and, even at this day, there are many portions of it which may be compared, not at all unfavorably, to country roads in Old and New England. In the mountainous regions it is often precipitous, and difficult of passage; but at such places it is provided with stone steps to relieve the worst hardships of ascent and descent. Wheeled vehicles cannot pass these points; but the To Kai Do was not made for wheels. Its carriages were *kagos* at the beginning; and the

To Fuziyama and Back. 131

use of more expeditious modes of conveyance was not foreseen or cared for. Those who wished for greater speed took horses, and rode according to their will. But, for the practical special purposes with which it was designed, the "East Sea Road" stands the equal of any similar work in any country. Who can wonder at the effect its hundreds of miles of spacious solidity and dexterous graduation produced upon the minds of the unaccustomed visitors in the seventeenth century?

At various points between Misima and Hakone, particularly where the road escapes from its usual seclusion of walls of pine, and skirts some bold promontory, tea-houses are stationed, with little observatories attached, to invite the traveller, and afford him the best chances of inspecting the outlying attractions of landscape and sea-view. Yielding to most of these temptations, we did not reach our destination until an unusually late hour; but our Yokohama attendants had preceded us, and the servant of the best Hakone hotel was on the watch to marshal us over the last inequalities of the route. The lake is believed, like most of the inland waters of Japan, to lie in the bed of a worn-out crater, down the sides of which we were finally hurried to its shores. The hour for investigation of any kind was long past, and active operations were necessarily suspended until the morning. Then the same good fortune that had followed us through the excursion brought a day of exceptional brilliancy. The lake was properly our first consideration; and our earliest cry, for boats and boatmen. Here, however, arose an obstacle which threatened for a moment to throw our projects into confusion. Boats there were, in abundance; but, owing to the lateness of the season, the boatmen had given over all anticipation of pleasure-seeking tourists, and had settled themselves to other avocations. One only could be found; and he shrank from the labor of propelling us over the whole length of the lake, and back, unaided. He was old, and apparently not over strong, and would not be persuaded or beguiled. For a brief and anxious period it seemed that we should be compelled to forego our aquatic scheme. We could not undertake to supply the motive power ourselves, none of us understanding the peculiar manipulation of a Japanese oar. Suddenly, our leading servant announced, that, though unused to the labor for many years, he could twist a paddle, in case of need, with any navigator that Hakone could produce. From that moment, we were at ease again.

I am afraid I have not hitherto done justice to the worthy qualities and diversified accomplishments of this excellent man-of-all-work. In fact, it was only within a day or two that he had begun to shine with the full effulgence of which he was capable. We had originally taken him with us in spite of some misgivings, for which he was himself responsible. When we failed to obtain the interpreter whom we had counted upon, he had presented himself in Yokohama, and proffered claims to our consideration, which, so far as we could know, consisted of much zeal, and ten words of English. He had himself declared he was afraid he should not do, but was prepared to try his best. Moved rather by the frankness of his acknowledgments than by any sense of his fitness, we adopted him into our *cortége*. His ten words of English gave him a sort of supremacy at the outset, to which he speedily vindicated a more substantial title. He was an excellent waiter, could cook at a pinch, knew the route thoroughly, and had a tolerable fund of information and anecdote in relation to the country through which we passed. But it was not until we left Subasiri that he developed his higher moral qualities. Up to that time, our party of four had included, as I have had occasion to mention, one old resident of

Japan, who was familiar with the language and the manners of the people, and who could guard our innocence against any snares of mild deceit, or deviations from pecuniary rectitude. At Subasiri we lost this mainstay, he being obliged to return to Yokohama by the most expeditious course. Thenceforward we were forced to lean upon our chief retainer. His first action was to buy himself a straw hat. He had worn no hat at all, before, in which respect he was not distinguished from his fellow serving-men. With the hat, he assumed a tone and bearing of decided superiority over those with whom he had been accustomed to make himself equal. He smiled more than ever when he spoke to us; but with his countrymen his demeanor was grave and distant,—not haughty or discourteous, but impressive. He exhibited a singular facility in the combination and comprehensive application of his ten words of English. From his tongue they really seemed to flow with a colloquial fluency not inferior to another man's hundred, or two hundred. He was partially intelligible almost half the time. He kept our accounts with scrupulous care, checked the premonitory symptoms of extortion which the innkeepers always manifested on finding that we were green strangers, awed the baggage-porters into submission whenever they displayed slight signs of rebellion, and in every way protected our interests with fidelity and firmness. Finally he perched himself upon a pinnacle in our esteem by divesting himself of his dignity in our time of need, and transforming himself into a gondolier. The least we could do was to bestow upon him a complimentary title, and so we called him Proteus. Moreover, we gave him a place in our memory, with other donations more directly applicable to the grosser requirements of his nature.

All these, and other things, being settled, we were soon floating upon the dark surface of Hakone Lake. And here, for the first time during our excursion, we were compelled to confess to a disappointment. The lake was not all our fancy had painted it. There shall be no denial of its many obvious beauties; but, on the whole, it could not strikingly affect those who had chanced to become familiar with the lakes of Switzerland or Italy. Perhaps its own extreme altitude (it is sometimes said to be the highest sheet of water in Japan, and is, undoubtedly, several thousand feet above the sea-level), which robs the surrounding mountains of half their imposing grandeur, may be to its disadvantage. Indeed, I afterward had frequent occasion to observe that the highland lakes generally were not to be favorably measured with those of Europe and America. Whatever the cause, Hakone was comparatively unsatisfactory. Its body was of a gloomy hue; and, as the occupant of a crater, it had no islands to vary its monotony. We traversed its entire length, some six or seven miles, to the northwestern outlet; then we returned, without enthusiasm. I do not wish to speak harshly of this aggregation of celebrated waves; nor do I, at this lapse of time, cherish any feeling of serious resentment against it for having failed to meet anticipation. Possibly, if we had come upon it before witnessing so many novelties and splendors, it might have touched us differently. The truth undoubtedly is, that we expected too much; but it is equally the undoubted truth, that, in respect of its lake scenery, Japan is not justly entitled to enter the first rank among nations.

The village of Hakone is a quiet and wholly unimportant little place, with barely a score of houses to its name. It has temples and bronze statues of some interest, and anciently of great repute; and it possesses a historical consideration from the fact, that during the period of the Tokugawa sway, from the time of Iyeyasu until the overthrow of the dynasty in 1868, it was the most strictly guarded of all the approaches to Yedo. No persons, no matter what their rank might be, were suffered to pass without suitable examination; and few women were allowed to cross the barrier on any pretence. It was the outpost of Odawara, which was designated by the founder of the Tokugawas as one of the eight natural defences of the Eastern capital. But the gates and guard-houses of Hakone disappeared with the last revolution, and we saw no trace of them, except their stone foundations.

VIII.

Our progress after leaving Hakone was steadily downward to the village of Hata, which enjoys a very high and well-merited celebrity among travellers of all nations. It consists of a single street, or, rather, it is made up of two rows of houses, which are built along the To Kai Do. There is no room for more. On one side the hill rises abruptly, and the other overlooks a deep chasm. This little line of shops and dwellings is famous in several ways. It is as full of industry as a beehive, and turns out an almost incredible number of small wooden-wares, — boxes curiously fashioned of a wood with rough white bark, which natural covering is left untouched ; trays ; small tables ; and toys of every description that can be made from trees. It clings to the side of the precipice in just the way to make it one of the most picturesque of all the villages in the neighborhood of Yokohama. And it has a dainty inn, of which all who have ever occupied it are rival eulogists.

This excellent inn, once more, in consequence

To Fuziyama and Back. 139

of the lateness of the season, was entirely at our disposal. It was not a spacious edifice, for such a thing is impossible in Hata; but it united, in its modest dimensions, as many good qualities as most taverns of a larger (even the largest) growth can show. It has a gem of a garden, containing a pond filled by a natural cascade, and quite a mimic labyrinth of paths and subterranean avenues. At the summit of one of its supposititious peaks is a pretty shrine, which appears to have been placed there for ornament — so far as guests are concerned; and for use — so far as the regular household are concerned. I certainly saw more than one of them offering devotional tribute to it in the early morning. Perhaps the most captivating feature of the establishment was its corps of waiting-maids. They were sisters, and three in number. Their names, as a matter of fact, were brief, and not poetic, — "Sin," "Mon," and "Kin," — as a matter of polite form these were syllabically expanded to any extent that might suit the courteous inclination of those who addressed them. They were young, blithe, and very alert; and the circumstance that they were extremely pretty did not impair their efficacy as domestics in the slightest degree. We talked to them with the greatest ease, and without the aid of an interpreter. They did not understand us; but that was a trifle which gave concern to neither us nor them. They sang to us, and played the light fantastic *samisen* after dinner. It was a lovely night. There were three of them, and there were three of us, which we justly regarded as a coincidence. They were the first strikingly attractive of their sex we had seen, and I think that some of us dreamed of them.

Next morning we explored the place a number of times. This was accomplished without difficulty, as it needed only three or four minutes to move from one end of it to the other. We watched the gradual growth of toys and ornamental ware under the nimble fingers of the craftsmen. What struck me as the most facile workmanship of all, though by no means the most delicate, was the evolution of rough sandals from a pile of rice-straw. The maker would grasp a loose handful, and, by rubbing and twisting it between his hands for a few seconds, would transform it into a thick cord, or small rope. A couple of longitudinal manipulations smoothed the surface of this cord, and made it ready for further development. Then the show began. I saw him take four strands, one in each hand, and one in each foot, — yes, in each foot, between the two biggest toes, — and begin to plait them. That is all I can describe with exactitude. It was impossible to follow his motions after the first moment. He seemed merely to tie himself into hard straw knots a dozen or twenty times, and untie himself with his teeth, and, lo, a sandal! When we applauded him, he looked bewildered.

We were in the highest possible spirits. The brisk and busy temper of Hata quickened our senses, and moved us to a variety of amiable demonstrations. One of our party succeeded in establishing friendly relations with a dog. This was no insignificant achievement; for the dogs of Japan, I regret to say, are of a very low moral grade. They are suspicious, morose, and intractable. They dislike all human beings, especially foreigners, and make no attempt to disguise their animosity. To win even a superficial show of familiarity from one of them was therefore a triumph. This single pliable dog consented to accept a pat, and to confer a wag. I had never seen a dog's tail wag, in Japan, up to that moment. What was more, he followed us several times through the village, not impelled, however, by sudden affection, but rather moved by curiosity, and apparently anxious to discover, through nasal examination, what there was about us that had diverted him for a moment from his usual morbid humor. We had better fortune with the polite inhabitants of our own species. The adult population smiled and saluted us whenever we passed, though they were too busy to be disturbed from their regular vocations. But over the children we secured a complete conquest by a brilliant *coup*. Among the manufactures of Hata is a kind of wooden whistle, which is, perhaps, too costly to be used at home, and is sent to the larger towns for sale. To blow a whistle is one of the instinctive propensities and brightest ambitions of infancy, all the world over. Having collected the entire juvenile population, we distributed whistles among them. The mountain air was straightway filled with shrill pipings of thankfulness and praise. The public laughed; the dogs withdrew from sight, growling; and the birds on the trees exhausted themselves in efforts of rivalry. In the midst of the concert, we took leave of Hata.

Why, we asked ourselves, as we walked down the rocky hillside, why should harsh destiny drag us from this place? Where could "the smoke and stir of this dim spot which men call earth" be better dispelled and forgotten than here? What was there that forbade us to adopt this tranquil village as our abiding-place forever? Why might we not advantageously devote our future to an uninterrupted sequence of such harmless delights as had occupied our last score of hours? Why not continue to watch the carp in the pond at the tea-house, listen to the cascades, wonder at the miraculous growth of sandals, encourage canine civilization, bestow whistles upon small boys, and be waited upon by successive generations of Sins, Mons, and Kins, to all eternity? In the discussion of these questions we became pathetic, until, finally, philosophy came to our aid, and comforted us with the reflection, that, in point of solid fact, a single month's devotion to the unaccustomed calm of Japanese rural life would probably have wearied us beyond endurance. It may be the most blissful condition of existence in all the universe; but the habits of Anglo-Saxon nature could never be held in permanent subjection to such restraints as it imposes.

A few hours more of the picturesque route which we had now come to look upon as a matter of course, in this region, brought us to the valley where Odawara lies, from which we had set forth a week before. From this point, we had arranged to vary our excursion by taking a boat across the bay to the Isle of Ye (Ye no Sima), which is ranked by all native chroniclers among the most attractive spots of the whole empire. Our *kago*-bearers left us with a regret which I know was unfeigned, because they had been receiving from us, for several days at least, three times their usual wages. To the trifling task of hiring a boat our handy ten-worded servant declared himself fully equal; and, indeed, in less than a quarter of an hour, he presented himself at the head of a procession of nine men, every one of whom, he contrived to make us understand, was considered indispensable to the comfortable management of a light craft in those waters. We did not believe it, and attempted to remonstrate; but soon discovered the futility of argument upon a basis of ten words, and submitted without further resistance. So far as we could fathom the reasons assigned for this preposterous superfluity of ship's company, a little apprehension was entertained on account of the roughness of the bay, which would compel an extra degree of attention and care in navigation. It was not clear to us, that, under such circumstances, any possible advantage could be derived from overloading our craft; but it was useless for us to say so; and, none of us having studied in the Ravel school of pantomime, we could not express our convictions by gesticulation alone. Naturally, we yielded, and we did not much regret it, after all; for the various characteristics of our crew afforded no small amount of amusement during the voyage.

Nobody ever embarks at Odawara without getting wet, on account of the high rolling surf. The Japanese sailors care nothing for this, as their clothing does not materially differ from that of the fish, their prey. We did not like it so well; but it was no part of our business, on an expedition like this, to take note of the few distasteful incidents which we could not avoid. After passing through our ordeal of spray, we shot out into deep water, and were presently skimming eastward with remarkable swiftness. The actual working of the craft was done by a couple of practised mariners. The other seven looked on, and sang. At least, they sang until the mast was fixed, and the sail spread, and the boat began to bound; then some of them declined to sing any longer. I shall remember that little voyage as an instance of the fallibility of first impressions, and the impossibility of fairly estimating character by a superficial exterior view. Among our nine seamen were two that had particularly attracted my notice before starting. One was a model of youthful strength and activity, — hardy, muscular, and handsome, the ideal sailor-boy of nautical romance. The other was ill-favored, dark, and lowering. He was not of the usual Japanese type. When I gazed upon him, I recalled the fact that certain ethnologists trace the race to a Malay origin. The ancestors of this forbidding creature were undoubtedly Malay pirates. Moreover, he wore a knife in his belt, which none of the rest did. But see what happens to the best-laid theories. Before we had been at sea, or, I should perhaps say, at bay, a quarter of an hour, my sturdy heart-of-oak lay curled up in a stupor of sea-sickness; while the corsair grew more and more exuberant with every tossing wave, and chanted briny melodies without ceasing, except when he was occupied in the endeavor to make some of the passengers comfortable by certain ingenious appliances of his own contrivance. As regards freedom from sickness, he was an exception. He and the two managing directors alone preserved their internal equilibrium. The others went to grief early in the afternoon, and remained there until we neared our destination. In this respect they were not a particle better than our servants, who did not generally pretend to be any thing but landsmen. I have always held a private conviction, that at least two-thirds of our

To Fuziyama and Back. 147

crew were no more sailors than ourselves, and that they passed themselves off as such solely for the chance of making a pleasure-trip across the bay, and getting paid for it into the bargain. Holding this view, even at the time, I refused to commiserate their sufferings.

In one particular, this voyage may stand as among the most remarkable on record. Perhaps I might be justified in calling it the most remarkable, without exception, of any in which American travellers have been concerned. No resolutions of thanks were offered to the captain. Of course, we wished to offer them, and it was one of the painful deprivations of our lives to be compelled to abstain : but the obstacles were insurmountable. No resolutions worthy of the name could be compassed in ten words of English; and our interpreter had only ten at our disposal, as I have more than once mentioned. As the skipper was a good skipper, we could not let him go wholly unrewarded; and, resolutions being out of the question, we determined to offer him, as the next best thing, a small sum in addition to his stipulated payment. It was received in a manner which gave rise to doubts in my mind as to whether, in spite of a host of English and American precedents, and notwithstanding the reams of paper that have been exhausted in panegyric of Inman, Cunard, and Pacific Mail commanders, a practical endowment of this kind might not be more gladly received, as a universal rule, than the common offering of unmarketable rhetoric. Captains are captains, whatever their differences of station or color may be; and I do not believe there is one of them that ever went down to the sea, who would not prefer an ounce of "solid pudding" to a pound of "empty praise."

IX.

THE last half-hour of our passage was in comparatively still water; and, before we landed, everybody was in capital order again, and the crew once more became a tuneful nine. The comely young peasant, as I now believed him to be, grew very demonstrative, and handled a few ropes with a great deal of gallantry; but the illusion was gone, and I knew him for a fraud. We disembarked on a little isthmus of sand which makes Ye no Sima a peninsula, when the tide is low. We were now in a district which is frequently visited by foreigners; and learning that the inns of the town of Katase, upon the main island, were most commonly occupied, we allowed ourselves to be conducted to one of them. This was a mistake, as we afterward discovered; Ye no Sima itself possessing far better accommodations. There is no more trustworthy rule of conduct, in travelling in the neighborhood of the foreign settlements of Japan, than to avoid the lodging-places generally patronized by Europeans. It is now an old story, but as true as it always has been; that wherever foreigners plant themselves, or circulate, upon the soil of Japan, demoralization and disaster spring up among the natives. They cannot even visit a summer-resort without spreading disorder and confusion. In proportion to our increasing distance from Yokohama, we had found comfort, cleanliness, and refinement. As we drew near to it again, the reverse of the picture gradually began to show itself. Katase, we were told, at one time had tea-houses that were in no respect inferior to those of more distant towns. They were now defaced, dirty, ill-managed, and extortionate. Rudeness cannot be easily found in a Japanese tavern; but here there was a kind of coarse familiarity and boldness of demeanor, on the part of the attendants, that contrasted very unfavorably with what we had been used to for many days past. It needed no special quickness of observation to trace this to foreign influence. The majority of those who have visited Katase are of a class whose vicious instincts might be held in restraint, by fear of the consequences of their indulgence, among their own people; but who, when fairly outside of social surveillance, are under no control of delicacy or decency. Their excursions are little better than riots; and their festivities are simply orgies, sometimes of the most brutal character.

To Fuziyama and Back. 151

It happened to be Saturday night when we reached this place; and we encountered parties in our own tea-house, and in others close at hand, that had come down from Yokohama to pass the Sunday, and the members of which were celebrating their arrival by thwacking the "coolies;" aggressively flourishing their sticks and whips; flinging the female servants about, and handling them with revolting grossness; and generally deporting themselves in a manner sufficiently offensive to the eyes of their own countrymen, and utterly abominable to a Japanese of any cultivation. The whole neighborhood had long before been almost abandoned by decent native tourists, and given up to strangers, with the result that we, in 1870, witnessed and experienced.

Ye no Sima justifies its name, as an island, at high water. And an island we found it, with the isthmus submerged to the depth of two feet, when we undertook to cross over to it in the morning. Under these circumstances, it can be reached only by the primitive method of bestriding the shoulders of a stalwart porter; and porters are always abundant, and ready for the work. The Japanese appeared to find little difficulty in accommodating themselves to this mode of transit; but for us, it was a dire operation. We were anatomically so long, that we were obliged to lift our feet to an unnatural height to avoid wetting them. This destroyed the evenness of our balance; and we possessed no means of exhorting our carriers to grasp our knees, and steady us. We had nothing to lay hold of but their heads, which might have been serviceable, if they had been firm; but their necks were as supple as swans', and yielded to each pressure in a manner which added to our peril, instead of fortifying us. Our struggles were like those of an imperfectly educated rope-dancer; and we were all tremulous with the strange exertion, and, possibly, with trepidation, when we landed. We were able to calculate at once, with nice exactness, the length of time that the exploration of the island would require; for we determined to limit the indulgence of our curiosity to the period of the lowest tidal ebb. One such experience was more, much more, than enough.

The island is chiefly celebrated for the noble view of Fuziyama which it affords; and, indeed, this takes rank among the finest scenic spectacles of Japan. But it has also, in itself, a number of notable attractions. Though small, it is lofty; and, although the coast behind it is unusually level, it presents a precipitous and defiant front to the open bay. Its rugged sides, riven by volcanic convulsions, and channelled by the action of the waves, bear a close resemblance to the cliffs of Nahant, near Boston. At its outermost extremity is the entrance to a cavern, which extends six hundred feet into the bowels of the rock, and the interior chambers of which are fitted up with altars and images, and used as shrines by Buddhist devotees. It is inaccessible, except at low tides; yet the priests seldom forsake it, and continue their functions undisturbed, on the higher level of the recesses, while the opening is nearly or entirely stopped. The surface of Ye no Sima abounds in temples of more or less spacious dimensions, all of which are now sadly faded and decayed, although their legendary glory, in the mouths of their votaries, continues fair and undiminished.

The accidental misfortune of our arrival at this place on a Saturday night, plunging us, as it did, into the midst of a pandemonium of coarse foreign revelry, led to an abrupt change in the final disposition of our route. It was so evident that the shore-roads to Yokohama would be overrun, on Sunday and Monday, with disorderly stragglers, that a consultation was held as to the expediency of renouncing the land entirely, and pursuing our course in the same craft that had brought us from Odawara. There were undoubted objections, the principal being the deprivation of witnessing many wayside scenes of interest; but these all gave way before the loathing excited by the prospect of too close contact with the graceless wretches who made the region hideous with their obscene excesses. Perhaps we regretted it later; but the decision was taken and proclaimed, and on a fair Sunday morning we again set sail, this time on a perfectly tranquil sea, and gave the hours to revery and reminiscence, until the busy hum from Yokohama's active streets roused us to the labors of disembarkation. The day had just closed in a blaze of sunset-splendor such as can be witnessed only in the Japanese purity of atmosphere. The bay was like a sheet of gold; the distant mountains opposite, as they faded from sight, were touched with every tint of the rainbow; the ships at anchor and the lazy pleasure-boats for a few moments lost their dull reality, and were transfigured into glowing phantoms. In the midst of this brief and delicious twilight we stepped on shore, all alike inspired with a thankful sense of the marvellous friendly fortune that had thus attended our blithe excursion, from the very inception, even to the moment of its genial ending.

A JAPANESE STATESMAN AT HOME.

I.

HOW it came about, that, in the autumn of 1870, a certain priestly edifice set apart for the requirements of the United States Legation in Japan, but long given over to neglect and dilapidation, was temporarily inhabited and vitalized by the republican consul then stationed at Tokio; and how I, the present narrator, happened to occupy it jointly with that most companionable functionary, — I am not here called upon to relate. It is sufficient that we did take possession of the forsaken and well-nigh forgotten premises, and that with us, in pleasant community, went to dwell an engaging youth, whose father — an officer of exalted position in the Imperial Government — had some time before consigned him to the representative American's care, to enable the lad to acquire knowledge of such foreign customs as it might be desirable for him to understand before setting out upon a Western tour. He had not been with us many days, before we began to recognize this little gentleman, Hirosawa Kenzo by name, as a genuine spirit of life and good cheer in the household. His brightness, his intelligence, and his unfailing good-humor always had a very genial and wholesome influence upon every person who was thrown in contact with him. I should hardly know where else to look for the same qualities of vivacity and gentleness, of exuberance and docility, which are almost invariably united in the youth of Japan. For these happy attributes, Kenzo was neither more nor less distinguished than others of his class; but constant companionship naturally led us to value them especially in him. How much we were attached to him we did not ourselves know, until, a few months later, the calamity which darkened his young life touched us so deeply that we felt he had gained no common hold upon our regard.[1] That merry autumn and winter at our temple of Zemfuku was crowded with lively incidents, in all of which our light-hearted associate had his share, and the recollection of which tempts me to stray from the purpose of this brief chronicle, even before I have fairly

---

[1] His father was assassinated on the 27th of February, 1871.

A Japanese Statesman at Home. 157

commenced it. But I resist. For this occasion, Master Kenzo must stand in the background; while his father, the Japanese statesman, commands attention in his successive characters of guest and entertainer.

We had not long been settled in the secluded district of Asabu, — of which Zemfuku is the centre, — when the consul, one of whose characteristics was a raging and uncontrollable spirit of hospitality, began to look about him for appropriate victims. Having, in due course, captured and surfeited all the desirable foreigners within his grasp, he sighed, Alexanderwise, for new appetites to conquer. Why might he not, he proceeded to reason, surround himself, from time to time, with native guests? A Japanese always enjoys a dinner, and a good host always enjoys the enjoyment of his companions. Conversation might be restricted; but the mouth has other functions than those of vocal utterance, and he was at least certain that those with whom he could talk but little could console themselves by eating the more. The simple question then remaining was, Who should inaugurate the new system? Who, indeed, better than our young friend's father? It would possess some novelty for him, it would gratify Kenzo, and it would afford us the satisfaction of finding our legs under the same board as those of a very lofty dignitary of the Mikado's government. So Kenzo was despatched one morning, the bearer of a formal invitation, and returned to announce, with high glee, that his father would not fail to report himself on the appointed day, and that he would bring with him one of the interpreters of his office to enable us to flavor the material banquet, to some extent, with relishes of reason and condiments of soul. This having been so satisfactorily arranged, the consul's unquenchable fire of hospitality began to blaze afresh. He invented a set of reproaches, which he unsparingly applied to himself, for having neglected to invite some friend or acquaintance of Hirosawa Sama, to keep him in countenance, as it were, and to make him feel completely and in every way at his ease. Luckily it was not too late. A swift *yakunin* was sent forthwith to learn if Sawa Sama, the head of the Japanese Foreign Office, would honor us with his presence, and so forth, and so forth. Oh, yes! Mr. Sawa would be delighted to assist in the execution of our prandial project. He also would bring an accomplished linguist of his staff to interpret to him the character and construction of the several dishes, lest, like the famous Boston advocate, he should dilate with the wrong emotion. The party was then made up; and I, at least, awaited the occasion with a vast deal of eagerness, for until that time I had never been brought into close relations with any Japanese of high estate, and no better opportunity of appeasing my innocent curiosity could possibly have offered itself.

Several hours of unusual labor on the part of all the servants attached to the establishment succeeded in imparting to the principal rooms of the mansion an aspect, which, though it could hardly be called brilliant or imposing, was certainly a shade less lugubrious than that which they were accustomed to wear. For reasons which it is not necessary to expound, the United States Legation in Tokio had for years remained in a chronic condition of disorder; and no temporary occupants, as we were, would be justified in burdening themselves with the cost of rendering the whole of it habitable. It was our custom, therefore, to make use of only a limited portion. But on this occasion we felt stimulated to the effort of opening and putting to rights one or two extra apartments. The sliding-doors were thrown aside; the dust of three ambassadorial *régimes* was extirpated; a few palsied chairs and tables were invigorated by strings or nails; and the cobweb which had for years cast a sinister shadow over the counterfeit presentment of President Pierce's countenance was brushed away. A couple of large braziers (called by the Japanese *hi-bachi*, or firebowls) served the double purpose of augmenting the show of furniture, and diffusing a mild warmth. As we terminated the preparations by scattering around a profusion of illustrated literature, chiefly consisting of pictorial weeklies, a rattling of distant screens, and a quick shuffling of feet along our matted corridors, announced the arrival of one of the guests. It was Sawa, miraculously ahead of the hour, — punctuality, as a rule, existing only in imagination among the Japanese, and, in their minds, taking the place of procrastination, as the real thief of time. He came in the most radiant paraphernalia of his rank; and, as he held an extremely high personal station in addition to his official position, there was hardly any limit to the splendors with which he might adorn himself if it pleased him. He belonged to the class of *kuges*, of whom there were less than two hundred altogether in Japan, and who stood next in degree to the members of the Mikado's own family. Though they were all comparatively poor men, the wealthiest and most powerful of the *daimios*

A Japanese Statesman at Home. 161

were compelled to acknowledge their superior state, and, upon occasion, to perform certain acts of homage before them.[1] I cannot say whether the extreme vividness of his costume on this occasion was exceptional or not; but, unless he had wrapped himself in a rainbow, he could not well have presented a more variegated appearance. His head was surmounted by the purple cap peculiar to state dress, and his feet were protected by the lacquered shoes which none of lower rank than a *kuge* could wear. Between these two extremities he was an opalescent mass of white, green, and pink silk. Perhaps the most singular effect of color about him was produced by the principal aperture of his countenance. Until a recent period, it had been the custom for the *kuge*, in common with all other noblemen attached especially to the Mikado's court, to blacken their teeth; but, the practice having lately been abandoned, the interiors of their mouths exhibited a rich chocolate hue, which still remains, indeed, and will not disappear until time shall have gradually effaced the stains. In other respects he was simply a stalwart, hearty, and merry-faced gentleman of fifty, which is rather an advanced age for active life in Japan.

[1] In later years, *kuges* and *daimios* have been nominally blended in one order of nobility called *kuwazoku*.

Not long after Sawa's arrival, and while we were all interchanging compliments through Mr. Ishibashi, — the chief of the numerous and clever corps of interpreters in the government service, — a folding-door was suddenly pushed aside, and, without announcement of any kind, there strode in among us, with alert and graceful step, the stateliest and most commanding Japanese figure that I had ever seen. Nearly six feet tall, he seemed almost a giant beside those of his countrymen who surrounded him; and the freedom of his movement and gestures was in striking contrast with the somewhat rigid formality which Japanese gentlemen are apt to adopt at first interviews. Kenzo's face lighted up with boyish pride at the impression produced upon us; and I was afterward led to suspect, sometimes, that quite as much of the admiration in which he held his father was bestowed upon his physical frame as upon his intellectual force. And it was not his massive stature alone that was calculated to attract attention. Another Eastern face so fine had not fallen within my observation. Portraits of him have since appeared in European periodicals; but no engraving from a photograph could give any just idea of his true expression. I know that the likenesses taken by Japanese artists were wholly wanting in the animation of feature, and especially the lustre of the eyes, which particularly distinguished him. In lively humor and gay spirits he was a worthy rival of Sawa, and the capital terms upon which we all immediately found ourselves was evidence as strong of their determination to be pleased as of our desire to entertain them. Whatever possibilities of rare attire Hirosawa's office might confer upon him, he certainly did not avail himself of them. His dress was simple and quiet, though evidently of the finest fabrics.

Hirosawa's career is not without interest to those who are curious in the study of Japanese politics ; and its tragic termination, not long after the slight incidents here related, showed the dangers, that, in the disorganization of affairs which followed the Imperial Restoration of 1868, were apt to attend a rapid elevation to rank and power. Until his appointment to the post, in the central government, which he held at the time of his death, he had always been in the immediate service of the *Daimio* of Chosiu, one of the powerful southern nobles who combined some years before to destroy the ascendency of the hereditary *Taikuns*, and who succeeded in establishing. in the Mikado's name, an administration of their own selection. His talents and energy made him conspicuous while he was quite young; and, although not originally of very high rank, he speedily rose to the position of principal adviser and first executive officer of his lord. Having won unbounded confidence by his ability and his devotion in this capacity, he was chosen to represent the interests of his master in the newly formed cabinet of 1868. All the *daimios* who had been active in bringing about the revolution sent their ablest retainers to maintain their influence at the seat of government, if not to participate in the government itself; and it was admitted that none of them was better served than Hirosawa's fortunate chief. The zealous retainer received at the age of about thirty-eight the rank and title of *sangi*, which is the highest that any Japanese not nobly born can hope to attain,[1] and was appointed a member of the *Dai Jo Kuwan*, or principal board of government. All this we knew by well-authenticated report; but that his prestige was so great, and his influence so vast, as to render his existence a perpetual peril, we did not at that time imagine.

[1] The highest during life. Posthumous titles of more exalted meaning are sometimes conferred.

A Japanese Statesman at Home. 165

II.

THE dinner, I am happy to say, was a success. I confess that I had viewed some of the preparations with apprehension; and the array of varying courses decreed by the head of our family had struck me as being dangerously long and ponderous. Excess in such matters is scarcely less to be feared than insufficiency. Does not one of the first of English critics admit that he could never have finished reading the "Faëry Queen," if it had come down to him completed? And what playgoer, however enthusiastic, would tolerate "Hamlet" in ten acts? As far as banquets are concerned, I have seen more than one the exordium of which promised brilliantly, but which, through inordinate multiplication of superfluous dishes, never reached a suitable peroration. It was well, however, that a maturer experience than mine had the regulation of this matter. When I remonstrated, the consul, quoting a phrase which was famous in Washington years ago, simply said, "The sequel will demonstrate." And so it did. It demonstrated the accuracy of his foresight, and, at the same time, the immense digestive superiority of the Japanese over that of any foreign nation whose alimentary processes have fallen under my observation. The pageant was as far as you can imagine from insubstantial; but it melted and dissolved and faded as if it had been nothing better than the baseless fabric of a Barmecide's feast. It is true that the merit of the meal fully justified its quick consumption. The Japanese cooks are preternaturally skilful; and ours, who had made himself master of culinary arts under the training of a Frenchman, was conceded to stand at the crowning point of his craft. But, for all that, when it was over, my eyes were fixed upon the not abnormally distended bodies of our guests with an amazement similar to that experienced by the children of the " Deserted Village " in contemplating their teacher's head : —

"And still I gazed, and still the wonder grew," etc.

To this day it is a mystery to me how they contrived, while eating so much and so rapidly, to talk as volubly as they did. The conversation rattled incessantly. The poor interpreters had the hardest part of the work to do; and I confess to a suspicion, that on one or two occasions, when

A Japanese Statesman at Home. 167

some particularly palatable plate was served, the eminent Sawa wilfully and maliciously threw out an extremely difficult remark to be translated, and thus prevented the luckless linguists from enjoying their full share. Did I formally introduce the interpreters? They were, first, with the *Kuge*, Mr. Ishibashi, altogether the most fluent English-speaking native now in the employment of the government; and, second, with the *Sangi*, Mr. Tanaka, attached to the Treasury Department. I give each of them the title of "Mr." because, like most of their countrymen, they take very kindly to that prefix, applying it not only to themselves, but rather indiscriminately to everybody of whom they have occasion to speak. At this very dinner, Tanaka had ever so much to say about the machinations and recent misfortunes of one whom he persisted in calling "Mr. Napoleon." But, notwithstanding here and there a trivial error of this sort, both these gentlemen certainly managed their part of the general colloquy with extraordinary ease and exactitude. The amount of information upon current American and European topics, which they contrived to extract and re-issue for their chiefs, was hardly less remarkable than the quantity of food disposed of. On the other hand, they declared themselves entirely ready to give us any intelligence we might desire about their own country; and although it is considered the correct thing by most foreigners to discredit the word of a Japanese on all points, and especially upon subjects relating to the internal affairs of the nation, I have no doubt they were sincere enough. For my own part, I have found very little reluctance among these people to speak about themselves. Their want of knowledge is commonly mistaken for diplomatic reticence; and their professions of ignorance are set down as straightforward falsehoods. It is, however, a fact, that few Japanese are familiar with the history, or even the geography, of any part of their islands excepting that to which they individually belong. The political conditions of the country have always been unfavorable to the acquisition, or rather the diffusion, of any such information; and, indeed, their system of education has virtually forbidden it. One illustration of a willingness to discuss what might indeed be considered as among their state secrets occurred quite aptly. Sawa related, and apparently, from the mirth he inspired, with a good deal of humor, how, on that same morning, Hirosawa had come down from the *Dai Jo Kuwan* to the Foreign Office, had confronted and opposed the entire body of foreign ministers, himself included, upon a question of external policy, and, after a prolonged discussion, had carried his measures, single-handed, and brought them all around to his way of thinking. And nothing could have been more delightful than to witness, during the narration, the contrast between the deprecatory ejaculations of the flattered *Sangi*, and the belying twinkle of satisfaction in his eye.

There were, indeed, many other amusing things to observe besides the avidity of intellectual and physical appetite which the guests displayed. Not the least of these was the watchful solicitude with which Hirosawa regulated his movements by our own. Sawa had long been familiar with foreign tables. He was at one period governor of Nagasaki, and there became quite dexterous in the employment of knives, forks, and spoons. But our other friend could not yet manipulate them with sufficient expertness to enable him to feel wholly satisfied with himself. He was even shy of his napkin, and would not unfold it until he had seen the host remove his own from its place upon the table. And he busied himself solely with bread a considerable time before venturing upon any experiments with cutlery. After he had assured himself by intelligent scrutiny, however, he soon caught up with his better instructed companion; but he was still on the alert to detect new points, and furtively scanned us all before committing himself to any serious operation, such as helping himself to mustard, or dissecting a chicken-wing. Kenzo was not displeased at being able to distance his father in this one particular, and exhibited his prowess by an amplitude of action and a redundancy of gesture altogether out of his usual course. So we had abundance of entertainment on our side, in return for that we were able to bestow; and right sorrowful were both of us when the repast came to its termination. At an hour which would elsewhere be considered early, — about eight o'clock, — our new friends declared their determination to withdraw; and a few minutes later they had passed through their kneeling retinue at the door, and were winding their way through our avenues, torch-lighted, like a line of twinkling *ignes-fatui;* the most conspicuous object being Sawa's gigantic umbrella, some six feet high, with a plethoric paper lantern perched upon its tip like a huge glow-worm, and throwing a ruddy ray over the whole of the retiring procession.

A month later we received a request from Hirosawa Sangi to accept the same courtesy in his house that he had enjoyed in ours. I think that was about the way in which it was put, although the rhetorical involutions employed have entirely escaped my memory. In delivering this invitation, Master Kenzo let fall a hint that his father proposed to have a dinner prepared for us according to our own methods; but Mr. Consul, who managed to fit his humor very neatly into the crevices of the Japanese mind, crushed out that project by sending back a message, that, if we found a foreign repast awaiting us at Hirosawa's house, Hirosawa should certainly have a pure Japanese feast the next time he should come to us. Logic like this was unanswerable: so we received prompt assurance that we should encounter nothing but the genuine and unembellished *tabe-mono* of Tokio.

Accordingly, on a bright and comfortable December afternoon (December does not mean winter in the American or European sense of that frigid word), we started in procession from the Legation; our little Japanese friend and I occupying *norimono*, which were then the only popular conveyance in Japan, and the consul perched more loftily on horseback. In advance and at our rear stretched the body-guards which the government considered itself bound to provide on all occasions, not only for foreign officials, but also for visitors of every degree. To those who relish a certain sort of pomp and circumstance, their constant attendance was no doubt a gratification. To all others, among whom I beg to include myself, they were rather embarrassing and oppressive encumbrances, although, on the whole, as amiable and obliging a class of young officers as could anywhere be found. I, for one, was never able to overcome my sense of the absurdity of being " under protection " in a community against which no protection was needed ; and I was always worried by a conviction, that, beneath the smiling countenances of the citizens, there might be hidden a sneer at the pusillanimous strangers, who, so far as they could know, never ventured abroad unless surrounded by an armed police-force, and whose apparent excessive precautions must have seemed singularly ludicrous among a population where aggressive behavior and unprovoked violence were almost unknown. But the government had its reasons, no doubt; and, after all, the companionship of *yakunins* was not really a very heavy burden of discomfort.[1] On the afternoon in ques-

[1] The attendance of guards was dispensed with in 1872, through circumstances which I had some hand in shaping. They had been necessary up to that time in consequence of the frequent false alarms raised by foreigners, whose absurd inventions were eagerly used to disadvantage of the government. With guards as witnesses, their wild stories could not always be made effective.

tion, they were, for a marvel, actually of some service, — pointing out a new and recently opened road through the castle-grounds, which none of us had ever traversed before.

III.

In due time we reached our destination, — a neat and substantial mansion of the class occupied usually by all high government officials, and by *daimios* of secondary rank. There is little exterior display in any of the Tokio residences: even the *yashikis* of the wealthiest nobles, those whose annual rice revenues, under the old *régime*, were equivalent to millions of dollars, being distinguished only by their vast extent, and by a somewhat massive, though not especially imposing, wooden gateway. Hirosawa's house was situated on the most elevated ground which the city contains, — upon the hill known as Kudan, just outside the inner moat and wall of the Mikado's castle, and facing a broad common, part of which is used as the public race-course. It is a fair type, in exterior, of the dwelling-places of gentlemen of advanced, though not of the highest, station. A simple but curiously constructed wall, of tiles cemented by clay, some twelve feet high, serves the same purpose of concealment as the ungainly piles of brick which screen so many well-known London houses from public view. The portal, when opened, is amply spacious, and forms a sort of frame for an interior picture, which is by no means unattractive. A well-paved and scrupulously clean courtyard is surrounded on every side by low-roofed edifices, in all of which the sweeping curves of Eastern architecture are prominent, and which are profusely adorned with skilfully executed, though often grotesque, carvings and other ornamentation. At its farther end is a large open vestibule, the steps and floor of which are polished like mirrors, and from the dim corners of which we see numberless passages leading to various parts of the extensive establishment. From one of these, as we approach, our host emerges, wafting eloquent gesticulations of welcome, and beaming with smiles, in a manner calculated to weaken faith in the value of all verbal greetings. Throngs of retainers linger, remote and shadowy, in the receding corridors; but by his side stands a brisk little gentleman, whom we presently discover to be an old acquaintance named Yegawa, another of the inexhaustible corps of interpreters controlled by the government. Through him conversational relations are forthwith established; his brisk, electric manner suggesting magnetic communication in more than one way. Duly removing our shoes, — for the floors of every Japanese house, let alone that of a *sangi*, might stand for emblems of perfect purity, — we thread a series of matted halls, emerging, after a while, into a comfortable sort of reception-room, through the open outer doors of which one of the most charming little garden scenes imaginable is visible. Here it becomes our duty to exchange the salutations of the day. Seating ourselves with more or less ease and grace upon the floor, we converse, not rapidly or brilliantly perhaps, but with most determined and persistent courtesy. The forms being new to me, I discreetly leave the burden of this preliminary flourishing to my consul, and watch with amazement and delight the complimentary game of "give and take" which ensues. The Oriental principle, in introductory courtesies of this sort, appears to be akin to one with which professors of that wily Western sport, "poker," may perhaps be more familiar than other representatives of a younger civilization, — the principle of "seeing" your friendly antagonist, and "going one better." The illustration is not refined, but it is apt. Let us look for an instant at a fragment of this crescendo dialogue, with its Ossa of suavity piling upon Pelion of politeness, and with, from beginning to end, a vista like that of Pope's traveller, of "Alps on Alps" of swelling and ascending compliment. It must be short; for such things, however skilfully maintained, cannot last for more than a limited period, and, if unduly prolonged, would perish from their own inflation, like a gorgeous soap-bubble, the thinness of the material having no power to resist the unnatural distension beyond a certain strain.

THE CONSUL AND THE SANGI.

BRIEF COMEDY OF MANNERS.

THE CONSUL	C. O. S.
THE SANGI	H. H.
THE INTERPRETER	Y.
SILENT OBSERVERS . . .	H. K. and E. H. H.

THE CONSUL. — We hope that Hirosawa Hiosuké has enjoyed excellent health since we last saw him.

THE SANGI. — We have always hoped that the American Consul's health has been perfect, and are now filled with joy to find that it is so.

THE CONSUL. — We have never ceased to remember Mr. Hirosawa's visit with feelings of satisfaction and delight.

THE SANGI. — We are flattered that you have taken the trouble to come so far to return our visit; but we cannot expect that our humble attractions will enable you to enjoy yourselves here as we enjoyed ourselves with you.

THE CONSUL. — We hope that Mr. Hirosawa will not wait again for formal invitations, but that in future he will come to lunch or dine at Zemfuku-ji at any time that it may suit him, according to his own convenience.

THE SANGI. — If Mr. Consul and his friend should ever find themselves in the neighborhood of Hirosawa's house, they must also make their way in without ceremony, or he shall feel justly aggrieved.

THE CONSUL (*playing the full force of his hand*). — In fact, nothing could please us better, if such a thing were possible, than to see Mr. Hirosawa sitting beside us, with his excellent son, every day and evening.

THE SANGI (*over-reaching his friendly opponent with a confident "call"*). — Truly, if this house were suited to the comfort of foreigners, I would insist that both of you make your home henceforward here, with myself and my unworthy family. [*Pause, with affecting business of bowing and hand-shaking.*]

THE CONSUL (*attempting a diversion*). — Nothing could be more charming than the situation of Mr. Hirosawa's mansion, or prettier than his garden.

THE SANGI. — The grounds of Zemfuku-ji are singularly beautiful, and far superior to those of any residence occupied by Japanese.

THE CONSUL. — Mr. Hirosawa has certainly shown extraordinary skill in decorating every part of his establishment. Outside and inside, it is a series of pictures.

THE SANGI. — Since we visited your abode, we have endeavored to improve our own by availing ourselves of the recollections of the perfect taste and refinement we saw there, and arranging our apartments accordingly.

A Japanese Statesman at Home. 179

[*A second pause, the consul "throwing up his hand," as it were, in utter despair of "raising" the last remark.*]

THE CONSUL. — Mr. Hirosawa will be glad to know that his son is improving in his English studies every day.

THE SANGI. — That is solely in consequence of your kind attention in directing them.

THE CONSUL. — Certainly not. He is remarkably quick and intelligent, and learns with truly surprising rapidity.

THE SANGI. — All of which he gains directly from the quickness, the intelligence, and the rapidity of acquirement which distinguish his scholarly American friends.
[*Prolonged pause, and indications of exhaustion on one side. Renewed bowing and hand-shaking, after which ex. om. into the garden.*]

The garden, or series of gardens, was not large, but was arranged with the usual ingenuity of the Japanese, and, most of the trees being evergreens, presented an extremely attractive appearance, although it was mid-winter. The various artificial ponds were all hidden by thick coverings of straw, placed there, we were told, to protect the fish from the cold, though upon what fanciful theory we were not given to understand. At the end of the enclosure we were introduced to a miniature pagoda, two stories in height, the upper chamber of which was a favorite resort of the statesman. From its windows, not only the best part of Tokio was visible, — the ground being, as I have said, the highest in the city, — but the peak of Fuziyama, now a glittering, blinding prism of snow, stood in distinct view. This spectacle, indeed, is especially cherished by all who live within a radius of a hundred miles of the beautiful mountain. Especially in Tokio it is the creed that "no gentleman's house should be without it;" and I really believe it is rather on this account, than for any sanitary reasons, that dwelling-places upon the hills of the capital, however small their dimensions, are more eagerly coveted than the most spacious *yashikis* of the lowlands.

While we gazed and admired, a somewhat anachronistic species of refreshment was brought to us, consisting of jellies so rich and sweet as to be calculated, one would suppose, to impair our appetite for the more important repast that was to follow, and tea of a rare and superlatively fragrant quality, carefully prepared, we were told, not with boiling, or even hot, but only lukewarm water, it being believed by many that the flavors of the very finest teas can only thus be preserved. Master Kenzo considerately informed us that we need not feel ourselves bound to eat much of the unctuous dish, if we preferred wait-

A Japanese Statesman at Home. 181

ing a little longer for dinner, — a permission which his father ratified with a smile, and of which we accordingly availed ourselves. We began to observe, about this time, that most of the immediate provisions for our entertainment were in some sort under Kenzo's direction; the head of the family looking down from a height of great good nature upon the youngster's various artifices and expedients. I think that one of the most remarkable characteristics of the Japanese is the tender indulgence lavished by them upon their children, and the reciprocal respect and devotion which they receive. There seems to be no system of discipline or training, as we understand it, or profess to understand it, among them. Throughout all classes, high and low alike, the treatment of the young is almost extravagantly affectionate and considerate. I do not remember ever to have seen one of their children punished with violence. And yet I should not know where to look elsewhere for equal good temper and docility. It has seemed to me that the early admission of children to intimate and confidential association with their parents, and the frank interchange of ideas and feelings in which they are encouraged, give an ease and an early development which act with equal good for all.

Certainly there is a great deal of natural dignity and manliness about the young lads, without any departure — at least, so far as a stranger can observe — from the modesty and simplicity, which, in their family relations, become them so well.

Not very long after the tea-and-jelly episode, there came to us, from a part of the mansion which we had not yet visited, an attendant of second or third rank, who, with prodigality of smiles and profusion of obeisances, delivered what even our unaccustomed ears knew to be the summons to the chief ceremony of the day. We gently sighed in unison, — that little hypocritical sigh, familiar wherever civilization has reached the point of "dining out," and which, I suppose, in New York, London, Tokio, perhaps the Fiji Islands, alike, is meant to hide the happiness that springs within us under an affectation of regret that the delights of conversation are thus rudely interrupted by the abrupt appeal to our grosser natures. In that sigh I discovered a new link in the chain of social sympathy that binds the East and the West together. But we turned without delay, and were promptly marshalled to our ultimate destination, — as neat and dainty a refectory as any pair of deftly-decorated Parisian folding-doors could disclose, although it

A Japanese Statesman at Home. 183

shone out upon us through nothing more imposing than a couple of half-opened sliding-screens. Evening was drawing near; and the interior was illuminated with hanging-lanterns, and also with a single lamp of foreign device, to which an entire alcove was especially devoted. The light at first was purposely dim; but we could see that the walls were hung with a number of the delicate and ingenious paintings upon silk which form so important a part of the embellishment of every distinguished Japanese household, and which here, as elsewhere, variously represented flowers, fruits, or animals of the country, with occasionally a mytho-historical sketch, in which the heroic and the grotesque were indistinguishably blended. Exquisite frescos and bass-reliefs, some sketched, some wrought in elaborate lacquer-ware and gilded bronze, adorned the little doors that conceal the innumerable cupboards and pigeonholes which abound, and from the prevalence of which in all Japanese houses, it might fairly be imagined that secretiveness was the ruling passion of the race. Odd corners, again, were filled with quaint images and statues of great age and rarity; and the floricultural fancies of the host were shown by the pleasure with which he called attention to a few curious exotics, most of them brought, he told us, from China. To all of these we paid due attention; but it is useless to conceal that our minds were chiefly fixed upon the neat table, surrounded by five inviting chairs, which stood in the centre of the room, and which, though bearing for the moment nothing more suggestive than a snowy cloth, we glanced at with some impatience, knowing it to be the stage upon which a new and unknown species of epigastric drama was presently to be enacted for our entertainment. In this matter of the table and chairs, it must be said, Hirosawa had evaded his promise to us. Such effeminacies are unknown in genuine Japanese repasts; but we were assured that the recognition of foreign forms would go no farther, and that the Oriental integrity of our food should be absolutely above suspicion. So we offered no protest, and disposed ourselves as requested; the host expressing a courteous regret that his wife and other members of his family were visiting their native province, and therefore could not join us. Probably he meant what he said; although I believe that very few Japanese men of rank were at that date quite sufficiently *en rapport* with foreigners to bring the gentler part of their households into close and free communication with them.

IV.

Dusky forms are seen kneeling upon the mats of many surrounding apartments; but they do not gaze upon us curiously, nor do they, indeed, appear vividly conscious of our presence. They are, we discover, simply men-in-waiting. Five of them rise, thread their way noiselessly among their fellows, and speedily return, bearing each a small tray containing our first course. The little dishes are all precisely alike, and are arranged identically. We mutually bow and simper, split our chopsticks apart,[1] and set to work, — our Japanese friends with ease and vigor, we somewhat hesitatingly, and not without misgivings as to our ability to turn the unaccustomed utensils to proper account. In fact, it rapidly becomes apparent that the sense of our hands of little employment is so excessively dainty, that, unless we invoke instruction, we shall be able to make no way at all. Frankness being absolutely necessary, we make a great virtue of it, and declare,

[1] Courtesy and cleanliness alike demand, in Japan, that chopsticks be brought to a guest united at one end, like matches. This proves that they can never have been previously used.

with perhaps needless vehemence, that it really is useless, and that, after all, we cannot do it, and that we must throw ourselves upon the consideration of our host, because we shall certainly starve unless we are told how to proceed. Candor begets candor ; and our beaming entertainer, just as if he were announcing a hitherto unsuspected fact, and as if we had not marked and enjoyed it all at the time, observes that he found himself in the same awkward position when he dined with us. And here Master Yegawa, the interpreter, develops himself in the quality of a humorist. As one of us is struggling hopelessly with his slender sticks, which seem to have an independent activity of their own, darting themselves anywhere but in the direction aimed at by their holder, and frustrating almost every effort to project them mouthward, Yegawa proffers counsel. " Imitate me," he says, and begins picking and pecking bits of food of all sizes with an accuracy of movement almost mechanical. As if anybody could imitate him offhand ! The result of the first endeavor to do so is a consul strewn with Japanese edibles. " No, no ! " says Yegawa with steel-trap smartness. " I said, ' Imitate me ; ' but you never saw me do that. You are wrong. Excuse me ; but you are wholly wrong, and always will be wrong

A Japanese Statesman at Home. 187

unless you do as I do ; " which, of course, excites a proper amount of innocent mirth, for we are in the mood to be merry, and easily moved to laughter. But presently, although we cannot twirl our sticks with any thing like the amazing rapidity of our tutors, we contrive to serve ourselves after a certain complex method of our own, and are enabled to ascertain the quality of what is set before us. First, we explore the contents of a lacquered bowl, which contains a delicate soup spiced with seaweed and aromatic herbs. It is weak, but otherwise commendable. Other dishes are constructed, with curious fancy and singular ingenuity, to represent miniature gardens with mounds and ponds, or fortresses with turrets and moats ; the effects of landscape and architecture being produced by skilful arrangement of thin slices of fish or vegetables, and variously colored rice. Each plate is a little picture. I observe, that although preserved fruits, boiled chestnuts, bamboo-shoots, and other partly ornamental and partly appetizing condiments are scattered about, the substance of this course is rice and raw fish. Raw fish! I distinctly recall a series of thrilling emotions during the first battle-scene at which it was ever my fortune to assist; and I know it is on record in the annals of Franconia that I, personally, once crossed the tree that spans the Flume; I once went up in a balloon, though not very far; and I have passed a night on a peak in Formosa, surrounded by hostile cannibals: these all were memorable sensations. But now, confronting and confronted by raw fish as an article of diet, I learn the full depth, breadth, and vastness of meaning in the word "courage," and gain a new interpretation of a phrase which I have often lightly used, but never until now completely grasped and understood,—"true physical and moral heroism." Shall it be done? Can it be done? It must be done! 'Tis done! And is it utterly revolting and untenable? Hardly so. Do I like it, then? Truly, not too well; but I willingly admit it might be worse, especially as it is deftly mitigated by pungent soy. I do not know its name; but it is like salmon in aspect, and in taste like nothing in my particular prior experience. It is soft and gelatinous; and, after all, the flavor of the thick sauce with which it is enriched is perhaps prevalent above every thing else. The struggle once well over, I feel that I have encountered boldly, and conquered bravely. No future possibilities have any terror for me; nor is there any further occasion for such uncomfortable emotion. This preliminary course having been partly, and only partly, disposed of, Japanese hospitality supplying at least three times as much of every article as is intended to be eaten, five other servitors shoot from their spheres, and, after briskly clearing the table, produce another assortment of finely wrought lacquer-ware and porcelain dishes, containing, this time, a thick broth not unlike a Massachusetts chowder, compounded of fish, prawns, small slices of chickens, and sundry vegetables, with subordinate plates of spices, confectionery, and innumerable piquant stimulants to appetite, which I could hardly distinguish at the time, and which I certainly cannot now remember in detail. Successive courses, each introduced apparently by five fresh attendants, — the extraordinary number of which led us almost to think that Hirosawa must have borrowed his Lord of Chosiu's retinue for the occasion, — made us acquainted with still other varieties of soups, and with endless changes of composite *pot-pourris*, which it is very fortunately unnecessary to enumerate, because it is impossible. It may be recorded, however, that no less than thirteen times the spaces before us were cleared away and refilled, each change being distinguished by some new form of sparkling fluid, — beer, champagne, soda-water, I can't say what not. The partiality of the Japanese for all liquors of a bubbling and effervescent character is remarkable. The foam of ale to them is ecstasy, and the froth of champagne is rapture. It is not the quality of the draught, but the "fizz," that engages their fancy. I have actually and positively known a party of Japanese *yakunins* to take with them upon a long country excursion a quantity of Seidlitz, which they mixed with sugar and water, and drank as a luxurious beverage. Thirteen times, as I have observed, we were called upon to practically honor our entertainer's bounty; and then, just when a dark despair and dread began to hover over us, we were relieved by a courtly apology for the meagreness of the repast, accompanied by a regretful apprehension that we had not enjoyed sufficient cheer. And here began another act of that fine impromptu comedy, examples of which I have given above, the theme this time being the respective merits of American and Japanese dinners, which was only interrupted by the entrance of five new tray-bearers (I'll swear they were entirely new, and had not before appeared), with pots of charmingly fresh and fragrant tea, and little cases containing native tobacco and the tiny pipes of the country. It was all over; and, metaphorically, we breathed more freely, although

A Japanese Statesman at Home. 191

in simple fact it was difficult for us to breathe at all.

"All over." Yes, as far as the material part of the entertainment was concerned; but there was yet one rare æsthetic luxury in store. A wave of the hand from the host, and a set of folding-screens, unclosed till now, is moved aside, revealing a score of the bright and pretty dancing girls known as *gei-shas*, whose vocation it is to attend public or private festivals, and charm the eye and ear with their saltatory and musical accomplishments. A dozen of these advance, and take their places for action; while the others supply an instrumental and vocal accompaniment. The particular ballet first executed has few complications, and little animation, judged by a Western standard. The coryphées confine themselves principally to four steps, — forward, with a half-turn to the right, again forward, with a similar turn, again the same movement, and once again; the last bringing them into precisely their original positions. This is repeated a rather surfeiting number of times, and is varied only occasionally by a sudden stoop, the right knee touching the floor, and the bare foot of the left leg darting forth horizontally, and disclosing itself in a momentary pink flash. The monotony is relieved, however, by the active expression of the faces, and the peculiar curving and gesticulation of the twenty-four arms rising and falling and sweeping through the air with harmonious regularity. The fact that the arm of the Japanese *gei-sha* is a thing of beauty is recognized and recorded. Next in order are solos, all by the youngest half-dozen of the party. Of these, the "fan-dance," with copious recitative, — incomprehensible, of course, — and a vast deal of pantomimic action, shows the various coquettish uses to which that indispensable article of toilet may be applied. Wielded by a Japanese adept, the fan is far more comprehensive in its capabilities than even a Spanish señora would make it. It has a vocabulary of its own, a telegraphy for every phase of flirtation, — warning, remonstrance, defiance, invitation, acquiescence, and all the rest, from the shy exordium to the yielding end, — each shade of meaning said to be well defined, and clear to apprehension. The fan-dance is an interesting *étude de mœurs*. It is followed by others, which prove how thoroughly mere bodily motion may serve, upon occasion, for the communication of ideas. Here is exhibited a living panorama of Japanese existence, — pastoral, mechanical, martial, marine, high-life, and low-life, in their different stages.

As a termination to the whole, the famous *jon-kina* is announced. This is a dance and a game of forfeits combined; and from the start it is evident that the stately formality of the earlier performances has been dismissed for good and all. The participants begin by moving briskly in circles to a well-marked but unvarying measure, singing merrily at the same time, and watching each other with a keenness, which for a while it is difficult for the strangers to understand. Gradually they betray an unexpected ardor; they grow excited, their song is louder, and their motions are more energetic. Suddenly a single girdle is unwound, and tossed into a corner, the dance proceeding without interruption. It then appears that the sport involves proceedings of the "follow-my-leader" sort, and that any deviation from the routine is punished by the confiscation of an article of dress. Girdles, naturally, go first. In a few minutes they are all in a pile upon the floor, and the released garments flow more freely, none the less so, as the movements increase in wildness and celerity. Presently, a sleeve is snatched away, and the upper silken robe falls from one side, and hangs only by the opposite shoulder. As yet, there is no cause for alarm, since an under-waist of red crape continues to interpose. But am I bound to go on, and tell how far these eccentric quadrilles, with their laws of forfeiture from which there is no appeal, are carried? Decidedly, I am not so bound. I pass rapidly to the close. The musicians cast down their instruments, and join in the finish. A last exaction of penalties, a final flourish of white arms, a quick crescendo of voices, a sudden, sharp cry, arresting every member of the corps with instantaneous abruptness, a brief suggestion of halls of antique statuary, and the Japanese *jon-kina* is ended.

Conversation of a somewhat languid nature ensued; photographic albums were inspected and discussed, — imagine, in the year 1870, a collection of family and national photograph albums in the mansion of a Tokio official, and all the pictures (views of rare scenery, portraits of eminent officers of state and lofty nobles, and the like) produced by native artists! — the curiosities of the various apartments were once more inspected, until at last the time arrived for us to take up our longish journey homeward. The parting salutations were strictly American, as far as we, the inhabitants of Zemfuku-ji, were concerned, but very Oriental as between our host and his interpreter. First putting on their swords with great formality, they swiftly dropped upon their knees, and bent their foreheads to the ground repeatedly; and, while they thus bade one another farewell within doors, the innumerable attendants of the household and our guards performed the same ceremony in the courtyard. Every requirement of etiquette having been finally satisfied, we pushed forth into the darkness, and began our homeward march. The bearers of my *norimono* must have found their labors more severe on the return than on the outward trip; but that gave me little concern at the moment. For an instant or two, I took a drowsy satisfaction in reflecting that the motion of my conveyance was favorable to digestion, and then sank into a profound sleep, which lasted until I was duly shot out at the door of our own temple in Asabu.

V.

THIS which I have narrated happened in December, 1870. At the close of the following February it was my duty again to visit the house on Kudan, but this time with a sadly different purpose. For several weeks the capital had been agitated with portentous rumors; and, in spite of the mystery with which the prominent political leaders veiled their proceedings, it was evident that the public peace was menaced in some formidable manner. Large bodies of troops poured into the city from the southern provinces; and the augmentation of the guards at all the government offices, at the residences of high dignitaries, and at the numerous gates of the Mikado's castle, showed that unusual watchfulness and precaution were deemed essential. But no serious event occurred until the morning of the 27th, when the community was startled by the intelligence that Hirosawa had been murdered, while sleeping, just before dawn. A band of some thirty swordsmen had broken into his dwelling, had hewn him literally into pieces, and had escaped before a general alarm could be given. The purpose of the assassination, even if it has been discovered by the government, has never been revealed, even to the members of his family. Many speculations were rife at the period; but none could thoroughly or satisfactorily explain the possible causes of animosity against a man whom everybody admitted to have been one of the most popular of Japanese statesmen, who was not known to have a personal enemy in the world, and whose official career, although active and energetic, had never been aggressive or arrogant. Whatever may have been the ulterior intentions of the conspirators, it is certain that the shock produced by this violent deed was so great as to check any further prosecution of their designs. The entire official population of Tokio resolved itself, for the time, into a species of detective force; and the unanimous zeal displayed in endeavoring to trace the perpetrators of the murder apparently drove every thought from their minds, except that of concealment. At any rate, no general execution of the suspected plot was then attempted.

Our little friend Kenzo had returned, only a few days before, full of glee and excitement, from his first visit to China. The blow was too heavy for his young spirit. I found him almost speechless with grief, yet compelled to control his emotions, since all the formalities of the grave occasion must be conducted by him, the heir, and now the head of the family. The obsequies of an officer so high in station as Hirosawa had been required to be conducted with minute and exhaustive ceremony, no detail of which could be regulated without his co-operation. It was a sorrowful sight, — our light-hearted companion stricken to despair by the overwhelming calamity, and oppressed with cares so far beyond his years and strength. But the severest part of his trial was soon to end. The funeral was fixed for the 1st of March; and from that time, although he would be obliged to remain closely at home for forty days, to receive, as chief mourner, visits of condolence, no active duties would be imposed upon him.

The burial ceremonies themselves were as dignified, as solemn, and as truly touching, as any I have ever witnessed. No forms of respect and honor which Japanese customs allow were here omitted. Hundreds of civilians, many of them among the highest in the land, all clothed from head to foot in white, followed the body to the cemetery; and a military escort was supplied by a regiment of Chosiu soldiers. The spot selected for the interment was upon the hill of Atanga, where only the remains of persons of eminent distinction are deposited. The rites of sepulture were fulfilled in a little temple at the base of the hill, after which the coffin was carried to the summit of a thickly wooded knoll, where the grave had been prepared. Here the entire assemblage passed before it, each individual prostrating himself for a moment, and reverently laying upon it a sprig of some consecrated tree. The nearest relations and friends knelt in a circle, and thus remained in silence until nightfall, when the tomb was closed, and all slowly withdrew, leaving every thing behind but the memory of Hirosawa Hiosuké.

A DAY IN A JAPANESE THEATRE.

I.

HE who would gain a just idea of the various qualities of a Japanese theatre — its conspicuous merits and its flagrant faults, its contrasts of rude simplicity and lavish splendor, its swift successions of dexterous illusion and awkward disenchantment, its alternating incongruities of genuine dramatic taste and skill, and reckless defiance of æsthetic and human proprieties — must give, at least, one uninterrupted day to its study, going early, and leaving only when all is finished. Repeated visits of shorter duration will hardly serve; for they will almost surely exclude some element, not only of entertainment, but also of importance in estimating the general value of theatrical art among the Japanese. In the performances of one day, fair examples will probably be found of nearly all that they attempt to accomplish. Unlike the Chinese, who are content to follow the course of a tortu-

A Day in a Japanese Theatre. 201

ous tragedy or complicated comedy through days and weeks of evolution, the Japanese must have variety, as well as abundance, in their mimic sports. Their more active nature requires the stimulant of continual novelty; and for the price of a single day's amusement, they expect, and usually receive, a complete Polonius's list of representations, with additional details of the kind referred to by Hamlet as more appropriate to the Polonial humor.[1] One thorough visit, then, will doubtless enable the foreign spectator to satisfy himself as to the standard of the Nippon drama, and to determine its rank among like exhibitions in other lands. If it recommend itself to his gentle senses, there is nothing to prevent him from repeating the experiment as often as he may choose: if it weary him, there is nothing to prevent him from staying away as freely as in any country where the form of government is supposed to be more liberal than in these islands of the Origin of the Sun.

Put yourself, I pray, under my guidance for a day, and come with me to Asakusa, at once the busiest and the merriest quarter of Tokio. Here, amid the incessant bustle of trade, are congregated the best of the public amusements which

[1] " He's for a jig," etc.

the great city possesses; most of them under the shadow of the majestic temple of Kuwan-non, which, unlike the majority of temples, is kept constantly open and in operation, perhaps as an antidote to the poisonous influences of concentrated commerce. Here are gardens, with quaint devices of dwarf forests, streams, and mountains, to tempt the curious. Here are archery-grounds, with nimble-fingered Oriental Dianas to fit the fugitive arrow to the evasive cord. Here are menageries, with nothing more ferocious about them than languid snakes and spiteful apes. Here are wax-works of truly marvellous fidelity, compared with which even Madame Tussaud's are commonplace caricatures. Here, also, are the theatres, — three of them, — keeping each other close company, as did once a famous row on the Boulevard du Temple. Of these we can take our choice. They are all alike externally, and are all sufficiently attractive to the eye, with gay flags protruding, and enormous lanterns depending, from their balconies, and their walls covered, like those of many play-houses at home, with transparencies representing the most impressive scenes in the favorite dramas of the day. It matters little which we enter. We pass the first, learning that it is already compactly full, and the second, because, although it is but a little past eight o'clock, the performance has already begun. At the door of the third, the proprietor, or his assistant, waits, bowing and smiling, to receive us, and, ascertaining which part of the house we wish to be placed in, precedes us to our destination, clearing the way, and making all comfortable before us, as an amiable usher would naturally do in any well-conducted American establishment. But, as regards payment, no word is spoken at this early period. That ungracious formality is left for a later stage. At present, the attendant's thoughts are occupied solely by his desire to bestow us comfortably in our box, with sundry cushions to mitigate the asperities of rough and angular boards, and with pots of fragrant tea to soothe the impatience of the interval before the opening of the day's dramatic budget. We may have chairs, European chairs, if we desire; but, of course, we reject them, as on such an occasion we would reject any thing unnecessarily alien, and, folding ourselves together upon the matted floor, we commence our personal proceedings by an inspection of the house and the assemblage.

It is certainly a plain and primitive edifice; thoroughly substantial, and neat enough, but totally destitute of any thing approaching to luxury;

covering a space about equal to that occupied by Niblo's Garden, in New York, though not equal to Niblo's in height; four solid walls bound together at the top by massive beams, and sheltered by a roof, the numerous apertures in which are so arranged, with broad shutters, as to produce specific scenic effects of light and shade. There is no ceiling, and, of course, no plastering or paint upon the woodwork in any part. The auditorial arrangements are not unlike those of the smaller French theatres. The centre of the floor is filled with stalls, or boxes, — the former name seems more appropriate here than it is with us, — square spaces separated from one another by partitions about ten inches high, each calculated comfortably to accommodate four, or possibly six persons. The aspect of the whole is suggestive of a magnified waffle-iron. Two aisles lead from the back of the house to the stage, which latter is not divided by any practical boundary from the body of the parquet, both being upon the same level. Indeed, these aisles appear to be intended rather for occasional exits and entrances of the actors than for the accommodation of visitors, the partitions between the boxes being sufficiently broad to afford an easy passage to the sure-footed Japanese. Along the outer side of each of the

A Day in a Japanese Theatre. 205

aisles a row of boxes, like the French *loges*, extends, constructed to hold four occupants apiece. The gallery — there is only one — chiefly consists of similar *loges*, the space in the extreme rear corresponding to the least select part of our playhouses. Altogether there is ample room for some twelve hundred persons, and, with a little of the pressure which American ushers are accustomed to exert, two thousand might be introduced without serious difficulty. Mats and cushions are liberally supplied; but no other conveniences are provided, or, indeed, looked for. The only decorations are a few colored hanging-curtains, stretching from side to side like our stage "borders;" rows of paper lanterns disposed about the edges of the gallery in the same manner as our gaseliers, and, like them, intended rather for ornament than use; and long strips of cloth thrown over the fronts of conspicuous boxes above and below, emblazoned with the names of popular actors, the crests of tutelary deities, and the titles of certain plays that have proved especially attractive. The curtain occupies the same position as with us; but there is no proscenium, and nothing to prevent the curious spectator from penetrating behind the scenes at pleasure, excepting his own sense of propriety. It is difficult to discover exactly what restrictions do exist in this respect; for even now, while the noise of preparation resounds, occupants of the front parquet-stalls occasionally lift the curtain before them, dart beneath it, and appear at the sides, having evidently chosen this speedier method of getting out, rather than a promenade along the somewhat narrow partition-tops; and little children, eager to explore the yet undivulged mysteries, leave their places, and, running down the aisles, peer curiously into the dim arena, unmolested and without rebuke.

Half-past eight o'clock (an unusually late hour), and the house is two-thirds full; but the performance does not begin. We have yet time to take observations of the audience, which, gayly gossiping, seems to care very little for the delay. Most of those present have come prepared to make a day of it, and a half-hour more or less is of little moment to them. The *élite* appear to be in the upper boxes, nearest the stage, although many fine dresses and aristocratic *tournures* are visible both in the lower boxes and the central stalls. On one side, far in front, there happen to be grouped, this morning, nearly a hundred children, mostly girls, inexpressibly bewitching in their pretty, gentle, innocent glee. I am never tired of paying tribute to the loveliness of the better class of Japanese children. As they sit there just beneath us, in their bright holiday attire, they form a picture which many a painter that I know of would give all his old pallets to get sight of, yet will not take a brief month's voyage to find. For a contrast, we may turn to the rear upper boxes, which are in possession of a body of pleasure-seeking soldiers, whose appearance is not at all picturesque. The Japanese *samurai*, in his transition state from nobleman's retainer-at-large to national guardsman, is as far as possible from an object of beauty. On entering his new military career, he is expected to throw off his former graceful but cumbrous robes, and adopt the garb of European armies; and he does this not unwillingly, but still awkwardly and by slow gradations. Instead of dashing boldly across the Rubicon of dress reform, he trifles on the brink, or plashes timidly and shallowly about, as if afraid of venturing too suddenly beyond his depth. The result is a series of the most extraordinary combinations that can be imagined, — fantastic hair-dressings, which refuse to accommodate themselves to the regulation cap; striped trousers rolled up to the thighs to relieve the legs from an unaccustomed and oppressive warmth; misalliances of the long-sleeved, flowing Japanese sack, with tight-fitting breeches (sometimes with nothing more than woollen drawers), and, *vice versa*, of the broad-legged *hakama* with close jackets; and in numerous cases, when all other obstacles have been overcome, a resolute adherence to the Japanese sandals and high pattens, which alone are sufficiently destructive to every pretension of military bearing, as we understand it. Valor, however, is not dependent upon accidents of apparel; and, if there is one quality which the *samurai* is known to possess in a higher degree than any other, it is that of indomitable physical courage. Behind the cluster of soldiers is a small gathering of neat-looking servants, apparently in waiting upon certain lofty *yakunins*, who occupy some of the best places in the house, and who are, in turn, attendants of a very distinguished officer, who sits with a small party in a half-hidden recess closely resembling one of those which, in old-fashioned French theatres, are situated upon the stage, behind the curtain. It is satisfactory to know that a recognized representative of Japanese dignity and mystery is near us; but the real interest of the scene, at present, lies in the body of the house, among the stalls, which are more heterogeneously filled, and spiced with

A Day in a Japanese Theatre. 209

more variety. How polite, good-humored, and sociable they all are! There are obvious distinctions of rank in dress; but, after the opening salutations of a conversation, there are none in intercourse. Though probably all strangers, they smile and jest, and puff one another's health in pinches of tobacco, and interchange candies and fruits like lifelong acquaintances. Candies and fruits! There is abundance of these: for no London pit ever resounded more freely with cries of venders of every known species of superfluous refreshment; and the trade they carry on is incessant, especially among the young folks, some of whom seem disposed to preclude all possibility of nourishing food, for that day at least, by surfeiting themselves with sweets at the outset. While we are amusing ourselves with the elaborate gravity with which these juvenile bargains are conducted, our friendly co-proprietor, or manager's assistant, or whatever he may be, comes to us with information that the real business is on the point of commencing, and hands us a package of programmes to prepare our minds properly for the delights in store, — to break, one might say, the artistic shock to us. Ah, these are indeed programmes! For amplitude of description, and copiousness of illustration, the new worlds of Europe and America know nothing to compare with them. They are not slips or sheets of paper, but little books, neatly bound, and worth preserving as ornaments after their immediate purpose has been served. They present a list of the day's proposed entertainments, with names of the actors and portraits of some of the most distinguished among them, followed by very full analyses of the various plots, with colored illustrations of the principal scenes. Apart from their usefulness in the theatre, they are said to be amusing little volumes for all occasions. It is true that a price is put upon them; but it is very small, — not more than a cent for each. As we pay for them, we learn also the price of our admission. This varies according to the hour when the visitor arrives; and, as we are among the earliest, no charge can be higher than ours. It is about two " *bu*," or half a dollar apiece; and if anybody can tell me where else upon earth you can go through so much by paying so little, I call upon him to deliver the information forthwith.

II.

THE attention of the audience is presently arrested by a series of sharp sounds behind the curtain, caused by rapping two hard and solid blocks of wood together, — a very common form of notification everywhere in Japan, and one which again suggests the French theatrical method of warning. After a dozen or more of these raps, three blows upon a drum are heard; and the curtain is rapidly drawn aside from the left of the stage to the right, revealing in the centre a neat and tasteful garden-scene, than which nothing need be more complete or more correctly designed. Less effective views and less accurate "sets" are often seen in more than one New York and London, not to say Paris theatre of pretention. The space occupied is small, — only about two-thirds the width of that disclosed by the withdrawal of the curtain, — and extending to what might correspond to the third entrance in one of our average sized houses; but it is well filled. Whatever other contradictions to literal fidelity we may observe, there is certainly none of that barbarous indifference, which, in Chinese theatres, allows the orchestra to be seen in full and noisy operation *behind* the actors, and demands no further concession to stage illusions than a portable bush to represent a forest, or a paper gate to stand for a walled city. The scenic appointments of the Japanese are quite well enough in their way; imperfect, of course, considered from our point, but excellent as far as they go. The disposition of their musicians, however, is open to severer criticism, of which, by the by, they are unsparing themselves, but seem reluctant to overthrow the old traditions, even while acknowledging their absurdity. From what would be their proscenium, if they had a proscenium, to what would be the edges of their first wings, if they had those, stretch two little galleries or platforms, about five feet above the stage, in which the orchestras and choruses are stationed. There are generally three *samisen*, or guitar-players, and three singers on each side; and it should be mentioned that one of the justifications of their presence in so conspicuous a position, is that the assistance of the choruses is supposed to be frequently required, to explain the progress of the drama. Their tuneful commentaries do, indeed, elucidate a great deal that might otherwise be obscure, and obviate the

A Day in a Japanese Theatre. 213

necessity of much dialogue and many soliloquies, which, without some such substitute, would be indispensable. It is easy to say that the whole system is ridiculous: yet who shall determine where the line of musical illustration is to be drawn? In many of our own melodramas, at least one-half of the action is sustained by orchestral accompaniments, and nobody disputes the value of such effects; and, if we attempt to apply logical tests, which is the more unreasonable, — for a chorus to tell us what is secretly passing in the mind of a particular character, or for that character to proclaim it himself in an outspoken soliloquy? And what mighty difference is there between being informed by three or four respectable middle-aged gentlemen, in melodious unison, that "an interval of two months is supposed, etc.," and reading the same upon a play-bill? The truth is, that there is no defence for either chorus or soliloquy, and not much for the impertinent and superfluous suggestions of play-bills: so we can afford to pass these questions unanswered. They need not, indeed, present themselves at all in this opening scene of the Tokio theatre; for we presently discover, that, before beginning the dramatic feast, a species of pantomimic prelude is offered, — intended, perhaps, to simulate a propitiatory appeal to supernatural powers, or, perhaps, only to introduce the more diversified proceedings of the day by an act of formal greeting to the assemblage. The regular musicians, all dressed in rich but plain-colored robes of state, having taken their accustomed places, the doors of a pavilion in the mimic garden are opened, and a dozen more imposing figures enter therefrom, bearing instruments which are not employed in the orchestras, though familiar enough to the Japanese ; namely, flutes, *kotos*,[1] and little drums of curious construction and various in tone, — some broad and shallow like tambourines, some long and slender, and some contracted like hourglasses. These gravely seat themselves in a row, as a line of chairless negro minstrels might do, and, without much delay, open a lively tournament of cacophonous rivalry with their neighbors overhead. The entries in the lists, however, are very gradual, and some five minutes pass before the whole force of twenty-four is in united operation. An hour-glass drum, perched lengthwise upon the player's right shoulder, and smartly

[1] The *koto* is an instrument resembling a magnified Æolian harp, the strings of which are sometimes stretched upon a hollow box, but generally upon a large block of solid wood. Its tone is soft and melodious, much more so than that of the *samisen*, which differs little from our banjo.

A Day in a Japanese Theatre.

tapped with the fingers of the left hand, is first sounded, the performer's voice following it in a monotonous recitative. *Samisens* in the galleries next emerge from silence, at first softly and timidly, as if afraid of intruding, but presently, gathering boldness, with a rising energy that threatens to extinguish the solitary drum, and calls for re-enforcement below, which is hastily thrown in by the wry-necked fife. A sonorous platform chorister soon mingles in the emulous fray, provoking a vigorous rejoinder from the entire body of vocalists upon the floor. The twelve above reply with a flowing phrase. The twelve below retort with a shrill stanza. Then all the drums are heard in a fine frenzy rolling, the *samisens* twitter, the *kotos* twang, and twenty-two pairs of lungs pour forth their utmost volume. Two flute-players alone, having their mouths as well as their hands full, and being unacquainted with the American art of singing through the nose, are forced to abstain from swelling the choral strain. But the tumult is sufficient with only their partial co-operation; and so, lustily and vigorously, for some sixty seconds, without interruption, the acoustic anguish is prolonged.

Suddenly, without premonition, and with no apparent cause, to inexperienced eyes, the commotion is multiplied by loud cries from the audience. Nothing has happened upon the stage to occasion such an outburst; but, following the gaze of the multitude, we perceive that two figures have entered from the rear of the parquet, and are now proceeding slowly down the aisles. The uproar of the populace is simply a demonstration of welcome. The actors are evidently familiar favorites; for, in addition to the usual welcome of cheers and clapping of hands, their names are shouted again and again by the more eager of their admirers,—a proof of extreme popularity. Unmoved by the applause, they glide majestically to the middle of the aisles, where they pause, salute each other and the audience, and then, in a series of easy undulations, their feet seeming never to leave the floor, move onward again toward the stage, having at last reached the centre of which, they stand motionless, for a few seconds, in attitudes of singular freedom and grace. By this time the general agitation is subdued, and tranquillity reigns again. During the next ten minutes, no sound is heard excepting the most gentle touches of the *samisens* and *kotos*, and an occasional cry of "Bando!" or "Danjuro!" — the names of the performers, — from some irrepressible enthusiast in the body of the house. Now is our opportunity

A Day in a Japanese Theatre. 217

for minute inspection. The characters represented are feminine; but the impersonators are men, as is almost always the case in Japan. As far as appearance goes, the disguise presents few difficulties; for it was until recently the custom of all women of position to powder their faces and necks in such profusion as to make the imitation of the artificial complexion an extremely easy matter. Certain prescribed touches of pink paint still further facilitate the masking of the countenance; and the hair, of course, is counterfeited without trouble. It is in the movement of the body and the management of the dress that the cleverness of the actor is shown; and in these details the couple before us are undoubtedly accomplished experts. Excepting their tallness, — and even this is not excessive, — there is nothing about them to betray their real sex to the most penetrating observation. Every trace of masculine angularity and stiffness has been banished from their frames. But these characteristics, which are afterward more curiously studied, do not at first strike us with so much surprise as the splendor of their apparel. Dresses more costly may sometimes be seen in Western theatres, but none at once so rich in material, so vivid in color, and so perfectly tasteful and harmonious in their extraordinary brilliancy. The chief materials are silk and velvet, of the finest Japanese quality, — which means the finest quality in the world, — overwrought with fanciful embroidery, and glittering with crystals and polished metals. The two costumes are at first precisely alike in form, but so contrived in color, that one seems a blaze of gold, the other a glare of silver. The head of each actor is covered with a tall shining hat, from which a fringe of bullion falls, entirely concealing the hair. The throat and shoulders are swathed with glittering scarfs. A long robe, with sleeves of inordinate length, is lightly bound around the figure, closing in at the ankles, and suddenly expanding about the feet, like an inverted lotosleaf. The waist is encircled by the broad Japanese cestus, or *obi*, heavily knotted at the back, in which are sheathed innocuous weapons and ornaments of various design. The combinations of color, and the effects produced by them, it is useless to attempt to describe: there is no proximate standard of previous recollection to measure them by. It is sufficient to say that past visions of "Black Crook" costumes, — I believe some of the characters wore clothes in that famous spectacle, — and those of similar displays, become dull and rusty in comparison. Moreover, one dress alone is not held sufficient for the occasion. A few stately gestures, and the hats and outer garments are thrown aside, disclosing a second and totally different attire, in no respect less striking than the first. And presently, after a haughty sweep around the stage, a third is unveiled, the most superb of all. The bodies of the two comedians are now cleared for action, and a dignified dance begins. I say a dance, although it exhibits little of the activity which the word implies with us. In the feminine choregraphy of Japan, there is no saltatory motion. The men are marvels of vivacity, but the women are always comparatively calm and subdued. Their feet do not appear to be lifted from the ground. They glide from spot to spot, with bodies rhythmically vibrating, and arms seductively swaying, pausing now and again, in postures of approved Oriental coquetry, to beckon with a fan-flirt, or lure with a smile. But of animated action there is very little, and here, this morning, less than usual, since the purpose of the performance is grave and austere, rather than jubilant and mirth-inspiring. Nevertheless, it is full of grace, and is impressive from the elaborate precision with which the movements of the two dancers are blended; and we willingly join in the acclamations which ring through the house, as, after a final swoop and flourish of prodigious expanse, they dart beneath the hanging-curtains of the pavilion, and vanish from public sight.

A Day in a Japanese Theatre. 221

III.

Now, amid the bustle which ensues, — hum of conversation, cries of refreshment-sellers, and rattle of machinery upon the stage, — we look to our programmes for what is to follow. "Bumbuku Chagama" is announced. "Bumbuku Chagama" is a typical dramatic subject in Japan, and shall therefore be explained. The literature of the country is full of fanciful legends and fables, — some apparently derived from foreign sources, and arbitrarily adapted to Japanese traditions; some exclusively national, and illustrative of such crude mythology as here exists. In the latter, the grotesque ideals of the fox, the badger, or some other mysteriously endowed animal, frequently figure. They are very old, generally very brief, and always extremely popular. Every child is familiar with hundreds of them; since they are circulated profusely in neat little pamphlets, drolly illustrated, at the cheap rate of about a dozen for a cent. Theatrical versions of these tales form about half the stock in trade of the Tokio playhouses. As we shall by and by discover, the dramatizations do not strictly follow the course of the original fables; but divergences of this sort have always been the inalienable privilege of play-writers, from Shakespeare down to the lowest. Among them all, "Bumbuku Chagama" is one of the best known and most frequently represented. Why this is so, nobody can satisfactorily explain; for it is only of average merit, and, as a mere narrative, has very little romantic or even human interest about it. But since it possesses a certain prominence, both as a favorite nursery fiction and an accepted theatrical theme, a double purpose may be served by offering first a strictly literal translation, and afterward showing in what manner it has been thought judicious to re-arrange it for dramatic treatment.

"BUMBUKU CHAGAMA;
OR,
THE BUBBLING TEAPOT.

"Once upon a time, it is said, there lived a very old badger in the temple known as Morin-ji, where there was also an iron teapot called Bumbuku Chagama, which was a precious thing in that sacred place. One day, when the chief priest — who was fond of tea, and who kept the pot always hanging in his own sitting-room — was about taking it as usual to make tea for drinking, a tail came out of it. He was startled, and called together all the little *bonzes*, his pupils, that they might behold the apparition. Supposing it to be the mischievous work of a fox or badger, and being resolved to ascertain its real character, they made due preparations. Some of them tied handkerchiefs about their heads; and some stripped their coats off the shoulders,[1] and armed themselves with sticks and bits of fire-wood. But, when they were about to beat the vessel down, wings came out of it; and as it flew about from one side to another, like a dragon-fly, while they pursued it, they could neither strike nor secure it. Finally, however, having closed all the windows and sliding-doors, after hunting it vigorously from one corner to another, they succeeded in confining it within a small space, and presently in capturing it.

"While they were variously consulting what they should do with it, a low merchant, whose business it was to collect and sell waste-paper, entered opportunely, and they showed him the teapot, with the view of disposing of it to him, if possible. He, observing their eagerness, offered

[1] Customary preparations of laboring-men for any arduous toil.

for it a much lower price than it was worth ; but, as it was now considered a monstrous thing in the temple, they allowed him to have it, even at the unfair valuation. Greatly rejoiced, he took it, and hastily carried it away, and reached his home well satisfied with his bargain, looking forward to a handsome profit the next day, when he hoped to sell it to some lover of tea-drinking.

"Night came on ; and he laid himself down upon his cushions to rest, and, covering himself with blankets, slept soundly. But at a later hour, toward the middle of the night, the teapot once more changed itself into the form of a badger, and came out from the waste-paper basket in which it had been placed. The merchant was aroused by the noise, and caught the teapot while it was in flight ; and, by treating it kindly, gained its confidence and affection. In the course of time, moreover, it became so docile, that he was able to teach it rope-dancing and various other accomplishments.

"The report soon spread that Bumbuku Chagama had learned to dance ; and the merchant was invited to various great and small provinces, where, also, he was summoned to exhibit the marvel before the *daimios*, who bestowed upon him large gifts of gold and silver. In course of time, he reflected that it was only through the teapot, which he had bought so cheap, that he had become prosperous, and felt it to be his duty to return it again, with some compensation, to the temple. He therefore carried it thither, and, telling the chief priest the story of all his good-fortune, offered to restore it, together with one-half of the money he had gained.

"The priest, well pleased with his gratitude and generosity, consented to receive the gifts. The badger was made the tutelary spirit of the temple, and the name of Bumbuku Chagama has remained famous in Morin-ji to the present day; and the tale will be held in remembrance until the latest ages as a legend of ancient times."

That is the whole story as it stands in popular literature. How it has been amplified and adorned for the stage, we shall now see.

As the curtain is drawn aside, we faintly discern the interior of a priest's apartment in the temple. The existence of an outer wall, toward the spectators, is, of course, left to the imagination; but a door is outlined by which the room communicates with a garden, the shrubbery in which is thickly laden with snow. It is a stormy night, and the effect of gloom is augmented by the closing of most of the large windows in the roof of the theatre. The wind moans, and the branches of the withered trees rustle uneasily. Upon the mats within, the chief priest sits or kneels beside his *hi-bachi* (fire-bowl), reading by the dim light of a large paper lantern. The iron teapot hangs upon the inner wall. The warmth and repose of this interior contrasts keenly with the restless discomfort of the scene outside.

Entering by one of the aisles, a huntsman advances, clothed in furs, carrying his matchlock on his shoulder, and his game-bag on his thigh. In pantomime he bewails the hard fortune of the day. The falling snow has extinguished his fusee when he most needed it. His fingers, cramped by frost, have failed him at the moment of firing. He has lost his usual steadiness upon the slippery ground, and missed his aim repeatedly. He is weary, cold, and hungry. All this is admirably told in silent action. Suddenly he discovers the light in the temple. He runs and asks admission. The old priest receives him hospitably, listens with interest to the tale of his misadventures, brings him cushions from behind a screen, and goes out in search of food, leaving directions for the huntsman to prepare hot water in the teapot.

A Day in a Japanese Theatre.

The gratified guest takes the huge vessel from its hook, and hangs it over the *hi-bachi*. A terrible shock awaits him. No sooner is the influence of the fire felt upon it than it opens in front, and a grinning badger's head protrudes. He recoils, awe-stricken and speechless; and, while he glares upon the apparition, it changes to a human countenance, — that of a young and comely woman. He springs toward it; but at that instant the priest returns, and the teapot resumes its ordinary shape.

Trembling with excitement, the huntsman hurriedly tells the marvellous story of what has happened. The priest attempts to pacify him, intimating that his brain is disturbed by hunger and exhaustion. The huntsman protests, but the priest is unconvinced. His scepticism, however, is speedily overthrown. He approaches the teapot to throw in the fragrant herb, when, lo! it vanishes, and in its place stands a blooming *musume*, all agitation and timidity, shrinking with sensitiveness, and cowering with confusion. The priest and huntsman, though greatly perplexed, are dazzled by her charms, and endeavor to reassure her; and she, coy and reluctant for a while, consents at last to be comforted. We observe that she resolutely keeps her face toward her entertainers; but, when she turns her back in our direction, we (the audience) discover that the beautiful young lady has a bushy tail. This piece of caudal confidence is intended to let us into the secret, that, in spite of seductive appearances, the fair visitor is in reality an imp of mischief, and still a badger at bottom. But the two victims are completely deluded.[1] The priest again retires, to fetch other refreshment especially suited to the delicate taste of his new guest. The huntsman and the beauty being left alone, flirtation ensues. From flirtation, the transition is rapid to ulterior consequences; and a succession of scenes is enacted almost as indescribable as some of those in Offenbach's "Gerolstein," or "Généviève." Incidentally the couple withdraw behind a large screen, which occupies a corner of the apartment, the action being suggestive of a familiar piece of "business" in the first finale of "Don Giovanni." The priest, returning, flutters, rages, writhes with jealousy. He is guilty of a meanness alike unbecoming to his character as a host and as a disciple of Buddha. He peeps through a crevice in the screen. What he discovers, or thinks he discovers, may be imagined from the fact, that, on the re-appearance of the mysteri-

[1] This trick of badgers and foxes turning themselves into women to mislead weak mortals is frequent in Japanese fable.

A Day in a Japanese Theatre. 229

ous stranger, he essays the military manœuvre of flanking her, and cutting off her rear. She is adroit and agile; but the priest, though aged, is animated by a triple energy. He is consumed by curiosity, his moral senses are shocked, and the fiend of jealousy urges him on. Moreover, the lady is so eagerly faced by the huntsman, that she has little opportunity for afterthought. The priest at length finds his opportunity, and seizes it; that is, he seizes the betraying member, — the tell-tail, if I may venture so to designate it. Then his eyes are fully opened. The disguise falls; and we behold no longer a woman, but a badger unadorned, an unpalliated ground-hog, an *ursus meles* unmitigated and undissembled. With the huntsman, however, the illusion is prolonged. He has still faith in the feminine fraud; and, while the priest is now chasing a four-footed fact with a bushy tail, he is pursuing a frolicsome phantom of his own species, with bright eyes, soft lips, and a dainty artificial complexion. The ardor of the priest at length prevails. The badger, incapable of longer maintaining its double identity, leaps once more into the teapot, which is grasped by the priest, and hurled from the window. The huntsman, with a wail of despair, flings himself after it; and the benevolent Buddhist, resolved to prosecute his good work to the end, also clambers laboriously forth, uttering cries of remonstrance and warning.

The scene slowly changes to a cemetery. Dusky gravestones are rimed with frost, and *ignes fatui* are flitting from mound to mound. The teapot lies upon the ground, as empty and desolate as the rest of the picture. It is evident that the badger has escaped. The huntsman runs in, looking from side to side, peering behind monuments, and listening acutely for his lost treasure. He espies it. It is there, half hidden behind a bush. As it moves swiftly away, he follows it. The priest appears, catches sight of the retreating forms, and starts again in pursuit. We may judge that he intercepts the fugitives; for he soon returns, driving the badger before him, and belaboring it with his lantern-stick. The chase is long continued; the sprite always showing itself in human form when the huntsman is near, and resuming its natural shape when approached by the priest. Before long, other badgers join the fray; and for a while we have a wild hunt of the "Freischütz" order, — a sort of Oriental Walpurgis witch-dance. But nothing can elude the persistence of the priest. Harassed and worn out, the original badger once more seeks refuge

A Day in a Japanese Theatre. 231

in the teapot. The priest, with the fragment of a tombstone, shatters the receptacle to atoms. As it breaks, some mysterious spell seems to be broken with it. The obnoxious animals retire, howling. The gravestones fall, and reveal flowers and pleasant architectural images. The churchyard is transformed into a smiling garden; and in the midst stands lovely woman, this time without a tail, as we are permitted to perceive, released from her enchantment, and ready to reward her adorer. He capers with glee; the priest beams benignantly upon them; and all ends as it should end, — abruptly, but happily.

IV.

THIS may serve as a fair description of an extremely popular though trivial class of Japanese drama. Of course, the supernatural element does not prevail in all; but it is very frequently employed, and is always heartily welcomed. We find, as the morning goes on, that lively comedies, and plays of the class which we call "domestic," are common; and historic episodes of political intrigue and warlike achievement are particularly favored, perhaps more so than the fables. One of the most agreeable to us — perhaps from the fact that we recognize in it an old acquaintance — is a pure fairy romance called "Momotaro," the story of which is a simple modification of our "Fair One with the Golden Locks;" the three friendly animals being, in this case, a pheasant, a monkey, and a dog. In all of them there is much to enjoy, something to admire, and a little to laugh at. The acting has more merit, and fewer faults, than we could have expected. In the portrayal of violent emotions, — of pride, terror, or rage, — these players could not be anywhere

A Day in a Japanese Theatre.

surpassed. Their truthfulness never wavers ; and, as a trifling commentary, it may be mentioned, that, during a certain ghost-scene, a party of children in the audience are so infected with the assumed fright of one of the actors, that they jump from their seats, and scamper out of the house in dismay. What is more, the actor in this scene, having fallen to the ground in an agony of alarm, and being obliged to make his exit at the moment, literally writhes himself along the aisle, and out of sight, in a series of convulsive throes, without once disturbing the illusion. He is upon the dangerous line of the ridiculous all the way, but he never oversteps it. In the gentler passions, however, they are less successful ; and we, of course, are not to be deceived by any serious love-making, when we know that both the parties to it are of the stouter sex. We scoff at sentiment when we spy a beard under the muffler. But in lighter comedy, or farce, this is a matter of less importance. And, truly, the fellows are astonishingly clever in their feminine airs and graces. As we saw before, the mimicry of personal appearance is perfect enough ; but an insurmountable difficulty lies in the voice. The Japanese actors do not attempt, like the Chinese, to speak in a strained falsetto, but maintain their natural tones ; and in this they are judicious, for, although they may not reproduce the real softness of womanly utterance, they at least avoid downright absurdity, which the Chinese never do. I am prepared to say, that, taken in a body, the Japanese comedians, as illustrators of the manners and feelings of their countrymen, are on a level with those of any Western nation. There is proof of close study and of genuine culture in all their performances ; and their most obvious error is not strictly a defect of art, but a defiance of nature. They complain, themselves, of the absence of women-players, and aver that they have often tried them, but have never found them sufficiently apt scholars. Perhaps they have not tried them with a due determination to make them succeed. Otherwise, they satisfy every reasonable requirement : and this, I am sure, would be the judgment of all, who, while examining their acting as critically as need be, would dissociate it from its embarrassing accessories. The illogical surroundings are what make it often appear irregular or grotesque ; and these are all really so extraneous and unnecessary, that they might be swept away at once, without disturbing in any degree the integrity of the representations. Put a company of first-class Japanese comedians upon one of our stages, and they might compete with the world, up to their limit of dramatic interpretation. Here, although they do not know it, they are needlessly hampered in a variety of ways. It is no excuse for anomalies like the perpetual jingle of orchestra and clamor of chorus, to say that others just as bad exist in other theatrical systems; and, so long as the Japanese actor has to contend against *samisens* and song-singers, he will always be at a disadvantage. The stage-arrangements, too, are ludicrously disregardful of the *ars celare*. The prompter usually stands in full view; and for the removal or introduction of furniture, or other properties, there is a battalion of lads-in-waiting, — gnome-like creatures in black, with crape veils over their faces, — who run about the scene, picking up a discarded dress, or supplying a sword whenever occasion demands. If a warrior falls dead upon the ground, after a combat quite as irrational as the "three-up and three-down" broadsword fights of our minor theatres, two of these attendants come forward, and stretch a shawl before him, under cover of which he rises and walks off the stage. Just picture the incongruities! After a passionate quarrel in which the rising wrath of each participant is depicted with masterly expression, a mock passage-at-arms ensues, which would not impose upon an infant. Receiving a death-wound, one of the duellists dies slowly and with a literalness of increasing torture which shows that he is following no imaginary model but has made himself perfect in the process by watchful observation, and immediately afterward jumps up and takes himself off behind a scarf which hides nothing. As to the scenic appliances, they are in most respects good, — more than merely good. There is no chance for broad effects, but the views are always prettily and elegantly painted. The method of scene-shifting is cumbersome, and wasteful of space, yet is not without a certain ingenuity of its own. The practicable stage is one large circle, which is bisected by the "flat," and which, being turned half around by hidden machinery, carries with it all that was in sight, and discloses an entirely fresh "set." The back of the old scene becomes the face of the new one. Sometimes groups of characters are thus made to disappear while their dialogue continues, and another body comes into view, laughing and chatting, more completely *in medias res* than is possible with us. Seen for the first time, this kind of change has a peculiar force. For other mechanical effects, the stage has plenty of traps, which are used for the ascent of spectres

A Day in a Japanese Theatre. 237

and spirits, for hiding-places in plays of intrigue, for secret passages in hostile surprises, and similar purposes.

The curtain having closed upon a particularly thrilling climax of bloodless carnage and animated death, our good-natured assistant manager, or something, who has hovered protectingly about us all day, comes again to the door of our box, and tells us, in a whisper, that the interval before the next performance will be long, and that, if we like, we may accompany him upon a short visit behind the scenes. This is indeed a privilege. We follow with alacrity, and soon find ourselves in the midst of that familiar confusion and disorder, which, I suppose, must always be the same wherever the theatre flourishes. One touch of the *coulisses* makes the whole world kin. Carpenters are rushing about, balancing heavy "flats" against the air, property-men are gathering together and redistributing their stores, and the stage-director is dancing diabolically around, execrating every thing, and generally deporting himself with the fury and ferocity, which, as is well known, are necessary to keep the drama from going to the dogs. Are we really in Japan? Why, this might be an *entr'acte* in any metropolitan theatre where pure English is supposed to be spoken. There is a degree of politeness prevailing here, amid all the hurry, which might elsewhere be thought to conflict with high art; but, in all other respects, we, who have penetrated these mysteries in many climes, are entirely at home. Our conductor insists upon leading us up stairs, down stairs, and into the actors' chambers, assuring us that we shall not intrude, but, as strangers, will be perfectly welcome. We are shown the windlass by which the stage is turned, the contrivances for wind whistling and rain pattering, the paint and property rooms, and are finally introduced to the presence of the principal players, all of whom, assisted by their dressers, are arraying themselves for the coming representations. They receive us very pleasantly, but are too busy to talk, as we well understand; and so, after a formal salutation, we speedily leave them. One gentleman, however, gorgeously clad in nothing but paint, whose preparations are quite completed, constitutes himself our companion from this point, and directs our attention to a number of interesting details. We remark that we have not yet witnessed any of his acting, but that, in compensation, we shall see a great deal of him when he does appear, referring, mildly, to his nakedness. He is pleased to catch the

A Day in a Japanese Theatre. 239

subtle humor of our jest, and he explains that he is to personate a *beto*, or groom, — one of a class which is distinguished all over Japan by profuse and elaborate tattooing ; and that he has been all day in the hands of a painter, who, as we see, has cleverly imitated the permanent decorations of the hostler tribe. In order properly to qualify himself as a *beto*, he has relinquished some of his best parts to other players. Is not this real devotion? Could the enthusiasm of that tragedian, who, as Othello, blacked himself all over, be carried to a higher pitch?

The sounds of the *samisen* warn us away, and we return to our box to find the stage cleared for a species of ballet. Numerous dances follow one another, — some very merry, some more subdued, but none so rigidly grave as that which opened the events of the day. Pantomime enters freely into this performance. There is a fan-dance, in which the omnipresent toy is put to more coquettish uses than ever a Rosina dreamed of. There is a shuttlecock-dance, the implements of which, like Macbeth's dagger, are but of the mind, but are capitally suggested by appropriate gesticulation. A favorite game with an elastic ball is worked into a dance ; and it is delightful to see with what mock energy the supposed ladies compete for the possession of the plaything, — which does not exist, — and, having obtained the airy nothing, how each one, in a stooping posture, chases it about, withholding it to the last possible moment from other claimants. There are plenty of dances by men as well, and they amply supply all that the women lack in activity. They have their own shuttlecock game; and the violent struggles they depict, the collisions and overthrows, the mortification at missing a stroke, and the elation when especially successful, are irresistibly ludicrous, particularly as there are no shuttlecock and battledoor all the while. In the same way, they go through the movements of the butterfly trick, of a certain dexterous feat with a looped handkerchief, and of vaulting exercises; the material fabrics being equally baseless in every case. Toward the end of this divertisement, an "umbrella-dance" is introduced, full of ingenious developments and strange surprises. The umbrella-dances which we have seen at home are stupid bores. Here the instrument is so contrived, that although, when shut, it is quite ordinary and insignificant in appearance, "with no points that any other umbrella might not have," when opened, it assumes, at the will of the holder, a dozen different shapes, colors, and dimensions.

The various combinations are thus made to resemble a brilliant pyrotechnic display. And the variety of uses to which they are put! Half closed, they are worn as high-peaked hats. With the handles bent, they are disposed upon the stage to imitate beds of flowers, among which the dancers promenade. Rolled edgewise over the ground, they become the wheels of a Harlequin coach, in which the queen of the ballet seems to ride. We really have seen nothing like it on any of the continents. The closing dance is not so entirely foreign in character. The women still retain their gentle stateliness; but, on the part of the men, it is a kind of raging cancan, worthy of the *habitués* of the Mabille, or even their coarser caricaturists, those female Bedouins of the stage, who, unsexed from the crown to the toe, figure in the modern English and American burlesque.

V.

It is now long past noon; and the exertion of long-continued applause, together with much laughter, has given us an appetite. We are informed that there are excellent tea-houses over the way; and, repairing to one of these, we find all that is needed for a satisfactory luncheon. This accomplished, we return to the theatre, taking with us sundry packages of choice Tokio confectionery, which we do not want, but which were urged upon us so cannily by a pretty waitress, that we found our command of the Japanese language insufficient to refuse them. There is yet a considerable time to wait before the renewal of the revels. A great deal of lively conversation is going on down stairs. The two-sworded *jeunesse dorée* are wandering about from box to box, shedding compliments, and collecting smiles. A little piece of business just beneath us seems to mean mischief. A young liberty-taker has made a loop in a long paper string, and thrown it, lasso-like, over one of the projecting hairpins of a tidy-looking damsel in front of him, obvi-

A Day in a Japanese Theatre. 243

ously intending thus to establish a cord of sympathy between himself and her. Nevertheless, though he pulls as firmly as he dares, she is not perceptibly drawn toward him. The surrounding spectators are greatly amused. We plainly see that the restraints of Western theatres are not recognized here; and, since larks are permitted and even encouraged, why should we not have one of our own? — by all means, an original, ingenious, spirited, and luminous lark, dazzlingly brilliant, but strictly innocent. We will lure from their nests below all the children that our own box and the two adjoining, which are empty, can contain. Unwinding the strings from our bundles of candy, we bait them with sugarplums, and cautiously drop them over the sides, not within the reach of those below, — we are too clever for that, — but just outside of it. The children laugh and clutch hysterically. Their guardians are convulsed; and, in fact, the entire audience thinks it about the best thing it has ever seen in its life. It is a magnificent popular success. We are only afraid that our friends behind the curtain may become envious. We beckon; but the children shake their heads doubtingly. They are not a bit afraid; but some of them think they are, and others like to pretend to be. They consult first together, then with their parents. The candy tempts them strongly, and so does the prospect of adventure. At last one little girl, a Winkelried in her way, runs up the aisle, climbs the staircase, and springs boldly in between us. *Rien ne coûte après le premier pas.* We are surrounded, stormed, and despoiled, before we can count ten in correct Japanese. It is more than a success: it is a triumph. We feel that a more flattering *début* can seldom have been made in this establishment. We are approved by the multitude, esteemed by a select circle of mothers, and adored by the infants, most of whom remain with us during the rest of the day, highly confidential and contented, and behaving as, I think, only Japanese children know how to behave.

The afternoon programme presents very little that is new. We have another historical sketch; a ghost-story in which a dreadful cat first as a magician destroys, and afterwards as an animal devours, an entire family; a comedy not long, but extremely broad; and a second ballet. As twilight approaches, and we are preparing to leave, we are exhorted to wait yet a little, and witness what the French call a *solennité*, — a first representation, and by candle-light; which latter condition is most unusual. Of course we consent

A Day in a Japanese Theatre. 245

to remain. Just before the termination of the ballet, a device well known in our theatres is practised. An actor, dressed simply as a citizen, rises from among the audience, and, attracting attention by cries and eccentric gestures, makes his way to the stage, having reached which, he changes his tone, and announces that his purpose was only to gain the public ear, and give information of the novelty in store, which is not set down in the bills. Everybody had risen to depart; but now everybody sits down again, and immediately after, we see, through the increasing darkness, an immense number of people pouring in from the street, who rapidly fill every corner of the house. It appears, that on the occasion of a first performance, which always takes place at the close of a day, the theatre is thrown open, and any person may enter gratuitously. This is undoubtedly intended to accomplish what at home is done by the newspapers. If a piece is well received, the favorable report of a thousand individuals is a good advertisement, and, indeed, is almost the only kind of public announcement possible in this place. As we have sometimes remarked in other communities, these free-comers are the most exigent of all auditors. While others are patient and calm, they immediately begin a series of clappings, poundings, and cat-calls that carry us back in imagination to Drury Lane on Boxing Night, or the Bowery in a bad temper. Before the stage-arrangements are ready, twilight has deepened into dusk; and, to dispel all doubt about the growing darkness, numbers of attendants proceed to render it visible by planting six dim candles along the line which with us is occupied by footlights. It is a fine specimen of what a notable emendator of "Paradise Lost" calls "transpicuous gloom." When the curtain is drawn, it is wholly impossible to distinguish any object; and it becomes a question whether we shall not have to content ourselves with colloquy, and imagine the action. But we have not yet fathomed the resources of the establishment. As the two actors who first take part in the new piece approach by the aisle, we see hovering before them a couple of will-o'-the-wisp-like lights, fastened to the end of long rods, and carried by a pair of the dark attendants before mentioned. Whenever a new performer appears upon the scene, he is preceded, and made partially distinguishable, by one of these; and when half a dozen are grouped together, the picture becomes weird and grotesque beyond description. This is so far outside the limits of possible illusion, that we cease

A Day in a Japanese Theatre. 247

to regard the representation as any thing but a curious experiment; and, even thus considered, it soon fails to be amusing. The mass of the spectators, however, enjoy it amazingly, and are quite indifferent to the abnormal and incomplete method of illumination. They follow the play — a short farce — with keen intentness, shake the edifice with laughter over its comic incidents, and break out in a frenzy of applause at the close, which gives the actors ample assurance of a new success. The long theatrical day is at an end. Lights are extinguished; and, with two thousand others, we blindly grope our way through intricate corridors, and down precipitous staircases, and emerge, with a sense of sudden relief, into the lively and well-lighted street. The last half-hour, certainly, has been a little oppressive; for the rest — I have my own conviction, as you may suppose; but one opinion, however sincere, does not make a verdict. May I have yours? And, knowing mine, do you think you can agree with me?

www.ingramcontent.com/pod-product-compliance
Lightning Source LLC
Chambersburg PA
CBHW031734230426

43669CB00007B/348